teen CUISINE

Matthew Locricchio Photography by James Peterson

S0-BNS-495

SKYSCAPE

▪ ACKNOWLEDGMENTS ▪

A cookbook is like a good recipe. If you make it with the best ingredients and follow the instructions, you are then proud to bring it to the table. Nobody writes a cookbook alone, and the combined efforts of a lot of people—the best ingredients—helped bring *Teen Cuisine* together. My gratitude goes to James Peterson for taking on this book and for producing the sumptuous photographs. To my editor, Margery Cuyler, for her vision, for having answers to my questions, and for her solid commitment to the book. Thanks to my copy editor, Andrea Chesman, for her unwavering attention to detail and welcome consistency (things I definitely needed). My sincere thanks also goes to Alice Piacenza for her smart styling who, along with her assistant, the amazing Sara Kaluzsher, made the recipe photo sessions so successful; to my dear friends Frank and Marna Brigtsen of Brigtsen's Restaurant in New Orleans and Charlie's Seafood in Harahan, Louisiana, for supplying authentic Po-boy rolls and teaching me the ways of the Po-boy. I am also so grateful to Kay Petronio for her perfect book design and Anahid Hamparian for her skilled art direction and her support throughout this project, and to Janet Hamlin, for her excellent illustrations. I would like to thank Nathalie Le Du and Ellen Aprea and the entire staff at Marshall Cavendish for their great efforts in producing *Teen Cuisine*. Thanks in addition to Brian Nadeau of Hamakua Farms, Ninole, Hawaii, and Rachel Samper, one of my recipe testers. Many sincere thanks to Jean and Rondi Brouwer of Blackwood and Brouwer Booksellers, Kinderhook, New York, for their professional expertise and munificence to this particular one author over the years.

Cookbooks have given me the rare opportunity to work with young chefs in schools, museums, workshops, and hands-on classes. They have proved to me there is a real demand for challenging recipes reflecting a new level of cuisine in the kitchen of young chefs. I am deeply grateful to those students who have inspired me.

Thanks to *The New York Times* columnist Julia Moskin who sent me in search of "real" macaroni and cheese.

To my sister, Joanne, my brothers, Paul and Anthony, my nieces and nephews in New York, Detroit, Connecticut, and Hawaii and their children—I am grateful to all of you for keeping me cooking and writing.

Text copyright © 2010 by Matthew Locricchio
Photographs copyright © 2010 by James Peterson Studio
All rights reserved

Amazon Publishing, Attn: Amazon Children's Publishing, P.O. Box 400818, Las Vegas, NV 89140
www.amazon.com/amazonchildrenspublishing

Library of Congress Cataloging-in-Publication Data

Locricchio, Matthew.
Teen cuisine / by Matthew Locricchio ; illustrated by Janet Hamlin ; photographs by James Peterson. — 1st ed.
p. cm.
Includes index.
ISBN 9781477847961
1. Cookery—Juvenile literature. I. Hamlin, Janet. II. Title.
TX652.5.L57 2011
641.5'083—dc22
2009046847

Printed in China
Book design by Kay Petronio
Editor: Margery Cuyler

SKYSCAPE

For R.K.F

Razz —
Merry Merry to you.
This is a belated birthday
gift fr the New teeny-
Bopper! Love you and can't
wait to see what you
cook up!.   xoxo Doobs
+
BooBoo

CONTENTS

TEENS: TAKE OVER THE VAST EMPTY SPACE CALLED THE KITCHEN!

You can shock the food world by successfully preparing tasty recipes at home. With so many excellent food options available, solid nutritional information at hand, and a real desire for cutting-edge recipes, you represent the future of world cooking. Here is a book that will keep you on top of the food scene as you refine your kitchen skills and try out delicious recipes at the same time.

Organic ingredients and foods are available in supermarkets from coast to coast. I recommend that whenever possible you involve yourself in your family's shopping and purchase local and organic ingredients. Don't have those options? Then shop for the best you can afford. Just decide what works for you and your budget.

If you buy ingredients grown nearby, you will experience the superior taste of local and organic fruits and heritage vegetables, pasture-raised grass-fed beef, line-caught seafood, and chickens raised with natural feeds. Eating organic not only ensures that the farming industry in the United States will remain vital to our economy, but it will allow us to savor the experience of creating real American dishes with products from our own soil. That's why I recommend using locally grown foods whenever possible for most of the recipes in this book.

Try to avoid mystery ingredients, partially hydrogenated oils, and the unpronounceable chemicals that are part of packaged or prepared foods. Foodies, food geeks, and cooking devotees unite! After all, you are what you eat. You do not need to accept plain and uninspired cooking in your kitchen. You can prepare and take pride in your own delicious dishes.

If you prefer recipes that rely on shortcuts such as canned foods, prepared ingredients, or microwave cooking, this is not the book for you. Some of my recipes are long and call for lots of steps. Some of them are quick and easy to prepare. If you enjoy the experience of cooking something wonderful, however, and want to attempt recipes that are both straightforward and challenging, then this is the book for you.

It takes practice to perfect culinary skills, but the time you spend learning how to cook and then throwing a party with your own dishes is downright rewarding and fun. When you hear the "ooohs" and "aaahs" of your guests, you will experience the joy of having made them happy with your cooking. That is the coolest feeling a cook can have. Dive in and see for yourselves if I'm not right. It's not just cooking, it's Teen Cuisine!

A WORD ABOUT SAFETY

- Wash your hands before you begin and when you are working with food. Washing under hot water with lots of soap for twenty seconds will greatly reduce the risk of transferring bacteria from your hands to the food. Wash your hands again after you handle raw meat, poultry, fish, or tofu.

- Wash cutting boards, countertops, and equipment with hot soapy water after they've been in contact with raw meat, poultry, and fish.

- Boil any marinades that were in contact with raw fish, meat, or poultry for at least 5 minutes to kill any bacteria from the raw ingredients.

- Always start with a clean kitchen before you begin any recipe and leave the kitchen clean when you're done.

- Read the entire recipe before you prepare it. You are less likely to make mistakes that way.

- Wear an apron. Tie back long hair so that it stays away from food and open flames. Why not do what a chef does and wear a clean hat to cover your hair?

- Pot holders and hot pads are essential equipment in any kitchen. The hands they save may be your own. Use pot holders, hot pads, and oven mitts only if they are dry. Using wet holders on a hot pan can cause a serious burn!

- Keep the handles of the pots and pans turned toward the middle of the stove. That way you won't accidently hit them and knock them over. Always use pot holders to lift a hot lid or to move a pan on the stove or in the oven.

- Remember to turn off the stove and oven when you are finished cooking.

KNIFE SAFETY

- Always hold a knife handle with dry hands. If your hands are wet, the knife might slip. Think of your hands as a team. One hand grips the handle to operate the blade while the other guides the food you are cutting. The hand holding the food should never come close to the blade of the knife. Go slowly. There is no reason to chop very fast.

- Work on a cutting board, never on a tabletop or countertop.

- Never place sharp knives in a sink full of soapy water, where they could be hidden from view. Someone reaching into the water might get hurt.

- Take good care of your knives. Chef knives should be washed by hand, never in a dishwasher.

BRILLIANT BREAKFASTS

SUNRISE MUFFINS

Nothing beats the excitement of a basket of homemade muffins set down in the center of your breakfast table. Sunrise Muffins say "Good morning" in the most inviting way. When preparing muffins, some cooks make the mistake of over mixing the batter, thinking it should be smooth. Lumpy is luscious when it comes to muffins. Is it breakfast yet?

MAKES 6 MUFFINS

4 medium-size carrots

1 orange

1¼ cups spelt flour or unbleached all-purpose flour

¾ cup whole-wheat pastry flour

¾ cup raw (turbinado) or granulated sugar

1 teaspoon baking soda

½ teaspoon baking powder

1 teaspoon ground cinnamon

¼ teaspoon salt

2 large eggs, lightly beaten

¼ cup molasses

½ cup safflower oil

¼ cup plain whole-milk yogurt

1 teaspoon pure vanilla extract

Butter and jam, to serve

6 paper muffin cup liners

6-cup muffin tin (each hole measuring 3½ inches in diameter and 1½ inches in depth)

On your mark . . .

- Preheat the oven to 400°F with a rack in the middle slot of the oven.

- Set the paper liners in the holes of your muffin tin.

- Wash and peel the carrots. Grate the carrots on the largest holes of a four-sided grater into a large bowl and set aside.

- Wash the orange. To make the zest, grate the outside of the orange on the smallest holes of a four-sided grater. Be careful not to scrape off the white pith underneath. Gently bang the grater against the bowl to release the zest. Measure 1 tablespoon and add to the carrots. Squeeze the juice from the orange. Measure ¼ cup and add to the carrots and orange zest. Mix together and set aside.

Get set . . .

- Combine the white and whole-wheat flours, sugar, baking soda, baking powder, cinnamon, and salt in a bowl. Mix together with a whisk.

- Add the carrot mixture along with the slightly beaten eggs, molasses, oil, yogurt, and vanilla to the flour mixture. Using a rubber spatula, lightly fold the ingredients together, until the flour has been absorbed into the batter. Don't over mix.

- Use a large spoon to spoon the batter into the muffin cups, filling each about three-quarters full. As you reach the bottom of the bowl, don't remix the batter.

Cook!

- Bake on the middle rack of the oven for 20 to 25 minutes, until the muffins are brown on top. Insert a toothpick or a wooden skewer into the middle of one of the muffins. If it comes out clean, the muffins are done.

- Let the muffins cool in the tin for 5 minutes, or until they have pulled away from the sides. Tip the tin over and the muffins should fall out. Place them on a rack to finish cooling.

- Serve with your favorite jam and butter.

CHEF'S TIPS

If you use a nonstick muffin pan, you won't need the paper liners. Lightly butter the muffin tins before you add the batter.

To fold ingredients means to blend lighter ingredients with heavier ones so that they are not over mixed.

This recipe will introduce you to spelt flour. Read more about spelt in the Kitchen Essentials section at the back of the book. Spelt flour can usually be found in most natural food stores and many supermarkets. Can't find spelt flour? These muffins will turn out fine if you use unbleached all-purpose flour.

FRESH FRUIT TOSTADOS

Tostados and fresh fruit have been dating for a long time. It's time they got together. Here is a perfect way to enjoy local, organic fruits near where you live. Pick what looks best at the store or farmers' market. This dish is a colorful addition to your brunch menu. An added bonus: your guests do most of the work assembling the tostados. How nice for you!

SERVES 6

FILLING
½ cup strawberry jam

2 tablespoons freshly squeezed orange juice

2 to 2 ½ pounds fresh strawberries, peaches, bananas, raspberries, blueberries, blackberries, kiwi, apples, small seedless grapes, pears, orange or tangerine slices, pitted fresh cherries

TOSTADOS SHELLS
2 tablespoons unsalted butter

2 tablespoons raw (turbinado) or granulated sugar

1 tablespoon ground cinnamon

12 (6-inch) corn tortillas

TOPPINGS
Fresh mint

Hippie Granola (see page 19)

Yogurt

Strawberry, mango, or lemon sorbet

Honey

On your mark . . .

- To prepare the filling, in a large bowl, combine the strawberry jam with the orange juice.

- Wash all the fruit. Peel, seed, and cut all the fruit into medium-size chunks as needed. Measure about 5 cups and add to the large bowl. Toss well to coat the fruit pieces with the strawberry-jam mixture.

- Chill the fruit mixture for 1 to 4 hours, but not overnight or it will get soggy.

Get set . . .

- Preheat the oven to 400°F with a rack in the middle slot of the oven.

- To prepare the tostados, in a small saucepan, melt the butter over low heat. Add the sugar and cinnamon and stir until the sugar melts. Remove from the heat.

- Lay the tortillas on a 12 by 18-inch baking sheet. With a pastry brush, lightly coat one side of the tortilla with the melted butter mixture.

- Repeat until all the tortillas are coated on one side.

Cook!

- Bake on the middle rack of the oven for 15 minutes, or until the tostado shells are lightly browned.

- Remove from the oven. Let the shells cool on the tray.

- Wash the mint, shake to remove excess water, and dry by rolling in paper towels. Coarsely chop the mint and set aside.

- Arrange the shells on a platter along with bowls of the chilled fresh fruit, granola, chopped fresh mint, yogurt, and assorted sorbets. Place the honey in a bowl.

- Invite your guests to scoop fruit onto a shell, then top it with yogurt or sorbet. Finish with a drizzle of honey and a sprinkling of granola.

HIPPIE GRANOLA

This crunchy blend of oats, nuts, seeds, raisins, and fresh fruit, showing off here in a bowl of milk, may be the perfect breakfast food. An original American breakfast invention, it was first called "granula" when it was a nineteenth-century minister's recipe for baked graham crackers broken into bite-sized chunks. It later achieved health-conscience hippie stardom in the 1960s and 1970s. This recipe will keep you moving past all those boxes in the cereal aisle and send you home to enjoy your own homemade granola. Peace and love!

MAKES 3½ QUARTS

4 cups (1¾ pounds) old-fashioned rolled oats (not instant)

½ cup raw almonds

1½ cups chopped walnuts

¾ cup sesame seeds

¾ cup sunflower seeds

1¼ cups unsweetened shredded coconut

½ cup honey

½ cup molasses or cane sugar syrup

½ cup safflower oil, plus 2 tablespoons for baking trays

1 cup raisins, currants, or your favorite sulfur-free dried fruit

On your mark . . .

- Preheat the oven to 350°F with a rack in the middle slot of the oven.
- Pour the oats evenly across a dry (ungreased) 13 by 18-inch heavy-duty metal baking pan.
- Bake the oats undisturbed for 25 minutes on the middle rack or until the oats turn a pale golden color and are not starchy to the touch.
- Let the oats cool on the baking sheet for 5 to 6 minutes but do not turn the oven off.
- Roughly chop the almonds.

Get set . . .

- Put the almonds, walnuts, and sesame seeds in a 10-inch heavy-bottom pan, preferably cast iron. Toast them over medium-high heat, stirring with a wooden spoon or spatula, for 5 to 6 minutes. Be careful not to burn them. The sesame seeds will toast faster than the nuts, so keep stirring to prevent burning. If necessary, lift the pan off the burner for a bit and lower the heat.

Cook!

- Mix the oats, toasted nuts, sesame and sunflower seeds, coconut, honey, molasses, and oil in a large bowl. Toss until everything is evenly combined.

- Generously grease two 13 by 18-inch baking sheets by pouring 1 tablespoon of oil on each tray and spreading it with a clean paper towel.

- Divide the oat mixture between the two baking sheets. Loosely spread out an even layer of the mixture onto the baking sheets, but don't pack it down. Place one tray on the middle rack of the the oven and the other tray on the next slot up.

- Bake undisturbed for 20 minutes. Halfway through the baking, rotate the trays by moving each to the opposite rack. The granola is done when it has started to lightly stick to the bottom of the baking tray.

- Remove the trays from the oven and set on wire racks for about 15 minutes. With a spatula, gently loosen the stuck bits of granola from the bottom of the trays, being careful not to break up the clumps. Let the granola cool completely.

- Pour granola from both trays into a large bowl. Add the raisins and gently toss everything together. Be careful not to break up the clumps.

- Pack in clean glass jars with lids.

- Keep cool and dry until you are ready to serve.

CHEF'S TIPS

If you don't have two 13 by 18-inch baking sheets, bake the granola in two batches. This recipe makes a large quantity of granola. It will keep for several months in tightly covered glass jars in the refrigerator. It also makes a great gift.

Don't be surprised if the molasses in the granola gives the milk in your bowl a golden color.

Try it with fresh strawberries, bananas, blueberries, or any fresh fruit on top. It is also excellent on ice cream and frozen yogurt.

PANCAKES

Pancakes have had many names—flapjacks, slapjacks, flatcars, hot cakes, ployes (rhymes with boys), and johnnycakes. They have been on the American breakfast table since the seventeenth century. Thomas Jefferson loved them and so did Ben Franklin. There is a pancake-day race in the towns of Liberal, Kansas, and Olney, England, at which women from both towns run down the streets flipping pancakes. The race has been run in Kansas since 1950 and is still the only race of its kind in the United States. There is also the Preston County Buckwheat Festival in West Virginia. This event has served a record 16,129 orders of pancakes and maple syrup to hungry fairgoers over a three-day love-fest for buckwheat. Here are two recipes, one that can be made quickly, and the other that needs to be refrigerated overnight to achieve maximum flavor. Happy flipping!

FAST CAKES

Did you just roll out of bed and want to whip up a fast and delicious pancake batter to serve for an unforgettable breakfast? Then this is the recipe for you.

MAKES 12 TO 14 (4-INCH) PANCAKES

DRY
1½ cups unbleached all-purpose flour

1 tablespoon sugar

½ teaspoon salt

½ teaspoon baking soda

WET
1 large egg

1½ cups buttermilk or whole milk

3 tablespoons salted butter, melted

Butter or canola oil for cooking the pancakes, plus more butter to serve

Maple syrup, to serve

On your mark . . .

- Preheat the oven to 250°F.
- Slide a heatproof serving platter into the oven.

Get set . . .

- With a whisk, combine the flour, sugar, salt, and baking soda in a large bowl.

- In a medium bowl, beat the egg, milk, and melted butter together. Add the wet ingredients to the dry ingredients in the large bowl. Stir until the ingredients just come together and the batter still has lumps.

Cook!

- Heat a griddle, heavy-bottomed frying pan, or cast-iron skillet over medium-high heat until hot, but not smoking. This will take about 2 minutes.

- Melt 1 teaspoon of the butter on the griddle.

- When the butter is hot and bubbly, drop the batter by spoonfuls to form the pancakes. Let it spread to make 3- to 4-inch circles.

- Cook for about 3 minutes, or until tiny bubbles form on the surfaces and the edges start to turn brown.

- Flip once. Cook on the other side for about 2 minutes, or until the batter has set and the sides of the pancake feel firm to the touch. Keep the finished pancake warm on the platter in the oven while you continue to make pancakes with the rest of the batter. Add additional butter or oil to the griddle or pan as needed.

- Serve hot with maple syrup and extra pats of butter.

SLOW CAKES

Buckwheat, the traditional flour for pancakes, makes pancakes that are surprisingly light. Slow Cakes need some advance planning so the batter can rise overnight in the refrigerator. You will be thrilled by how good these old-fashioned pancakes taste, and so will everyone who joins you around the breakfast table.

MAKES 20 TO 24 PANCAKES

2½ cups buckwheat flour or unbleached all-purpose flour

1 teaspoon salt

1 (¼-ounce) package active Rapid-rise yeast

2¼ cups warm water

2 tablespoons molasses

1½ tablespoons salted butter

¼ teaspoon baking soda

Canola oil for cooking the pancakes

Butter, to serve

Maple syrup, to serve

On your mark . . .

- With a whisk, combine the flour and salt in a large bowl.

- In a separate bowl, dissolve the yeast in 2 cups of the warm water. (The final ¼ cup of water is added at the end of the recipe.)

- Pour the yeast mixture into the flour. Add the molasses and stir into a thick batter. Do not over mix.

- Cover the bowl with aluminum foil and let the batter stand at room temperature for 1 hour. Set a timer so you don't forget.

- Refrigerate the batter, covered, overnight.

Get set . . .

- Remove the batter from the refrigerator.

- Melt the butter over low heat. Stir the butter into the batter.

- Stir in the baking soda. Add the final ¼ cup of water and mix into the batter.

Cook!

- Preheat the oven to 200°F with a rack in the middle slot of the oven.

- Slide a heatproof serving platter in the oven on the middle rack.

- Heat a griddle, heavy-bottomed frying pan, or cast-iron skillet over medium-high heat until hot but not smoking. This will take about 2 minutes.

- Spread about 1 teaspoon of oil on the griddle. When the oil is hot and bubbly, drop the batter by spoonfuls onto the griddle or pan to form the pancakes. Let it spread to make 3- to 4-inch circles.

- Let cook undisturbed for about 2 minutes, or until tiny bubbles form on the surfaces and the edges stiffen and start to brown.

- Flip once and cook on the other side for about 2 minutes, or until the batter has set and the center of the pancake feels slightly firm to the touch.

- To prevent the cooked pancakes from getting soggy, lay a folded dish towel on the platter in the oven and set the cooked pancakes on the towel. Cover with a cloth.

- Continue to make pancakes with the remaining batter, adding the cooked pancakes to the platter in the oven.

- Serve hot with maple syrup and pats of extra butter.

CHEF'S TIPS

Buckwheat flour is available in the health food section of your supermarket or in specialty stores that carry a variety of flours. Buckwheat is not really a grain; it is actually an herb and is a cousin to rhubarb and sorrel. It is packed with essential amino acids and B vitamins.

Rapid-rise yeast is a type of instant yeast. Depending on the brand, it may be called Fast Rising, Rapid Rise, Quick Rise, and/or Bread Machine Yeast.

SANTA FE TOFU SCRAMBLER

As a sensible and tasty substitute for eggs, this dish has gained a huge following among breakfast lovers. If you're ever in Santa Fe, and it's time to order breakfast, you might be asked, "Do you want Christmas?" That means "Do you want red and green salsa on top?" You should answer "yes," because it's too hard to choose just one. The following recipe will make you fall in love with tofu and experience a taste of Santa Fe at the same time.

SERVES 4

1 pound extra-firm, smoked tofu

1 tablespoon soy sauce

1 teaspoon chile powder

1 medium red onion

1 clove garlic

4 ounces fresh mushrooms (about 1 cup)

2 medium-size plum tomatoes

1 tablespoon extra-virgin olive oil

½ teaspoon ground turmeric

½ cup lightly packed grated Monterey Jack or cheddar cheese

¼ cup Red Salsa (see page 31) or your favorite store-bought

¼ cup Green Salsa (see page 30) or your favorite store-bought

Warm tortillas or whole-grain toast, to serve

On your mark . . .

- Rinse the tofu under cold water. Pat it dry with paper towels.

- Break it into large chunks over a medium-size bowl.

- Add the soy sauce and chile powder and toss well. Be careful not to break up the tofu chunks too much.

- Set the tofu aside for 10 to 15 minutes. The tofu mixture can be refrigerated for up to 3 hours.

Get set . . .

- Peel and chop the onion into small chunks. Place in a small bowl and set aside.

- Slightly crush the garlic by laying the flat side of a chef's knife on the clove and pressing firmly to break open the skin. Remove the skin, cut off the root end, and discard.

- Brush any dirt off the mushrooms with a paper towel. Do not wash the mushrooms or they will soak up water like a sponge and make for a very soggy finished dish. Gently pull out the stem in the mushroom cap and discard. Thinly slice the mushrooms. Place in another small bowl and set aside.

- Wash the tomatoes; cut out the stem circle at the top and discard. Coarsely chop the tomatoes and set aside

Cook!

- Heat the olive oil in a 10-inch heavy-bottomed frying pan or cast-iron skillet over medium-high heat.

- When the pan is hot but not smoking, add the onions and garlic. Sauté until the onions are soft and translucent. This will take about 4 minutes.

- Add the tomatoes and mushrooms. Sauté for 5 minutes or until the mushrooms are soft and the tomato juices thicken. Stir frequently to prevent burning and sticking.

- Add the tofu mixture and turmeric. Cook for another 6 to 8 minutes or until most of the liquid has cooked away. Use a spatula to scrape the bottom of the pan to release all the stuck bits.

- Stir in the cheese and cook until just melted.

- Spoon the scramble onto a serving platter and spread the red salsa and green salsa over each half. Pass warm tortillas or whole-grain toast at the table and serve the scramble hot.

CHEF'S TIP

Tofu comes in different textures and assorted flavors. If you can't find smoked, as called for in the recipe, you can use plain tofu, or pick the flavor that best suits you. Tofu is perishable. It must be refrigerated until you are ready to use it. Choose the freshness date on the package that is the furthest from the date you purchase it.

GREEN SALSA

Green Salsa is as versatile as it is spicy, and it is a great make-ahead recipe to have on hand. Use it on your Santa Fe Tofu Scrambler (see page 27) with tortilla chips, or whenever you want a delicious tasty pick-up to your dishes.

SERVES 6

2 cloves garlic

½ small white onion

1 pound tomatillos

8 to 10 cilantro sprigs

1 to 2 jalapeño peppers

3 cups water

2 teaspoons salt

1 tablespoon corn or canola oil

Tortilla chips or Santa Fe Scrambler (see page 27), to serve

On your mark, get set . . .

- Peel the garlic and leave whole.

- Peel the onion. Chop into small pieces and set aside.

- Peel off the papery husks from the tomatillos and discard. Wash the tomatillos with cold water.

- Wash the cilantro, shake to remove excess water, dry by rolling in paper towels, and set aside.

- Wash the jalapeños and set aside.

Cook!

- Combine the water, salt, garlic cloves, tomatillos, and whole jalapeños in a 3-quart saucepan.

- Bring the water to a boil over medium-high heat. Decrease the heat to low and simmer, uncovered, for 10 minutes.

- Drain the mixture in a colander, reserving ½ cup of the cooking liquid in a small bowl. Transfer the tomatillo mixture, cilantro, and reserved cooking liquid to the jar of a blender.

- Press the lid almost completely in place, but leave the lid slightly ajar. Blend at low speed for a few seconds. Now press the lid firmly in place and blend at high speed for 10 to 15 seconds, or until liquefied.

- Remove the jar from the blender and set near the stove.

- Heat the oil in a 10-inch heavy-bottomed frying pan or cast-iron skillet over medium heat for about 30 seconds.

- Add the chopped onion. Cook for 4 to 5 minutes, until the onion becomes soft and translucent.

- Remove the pan from the heat and pour in the mixture from the blender. Have a lid close by, as the mixture will bubble and boil when it hits the hot pan. Cover the pan with the lid to prevent spattering.

- Remove the cover and cook over low heat for about 5 minutes, stirring occasionally.

- Let it cool completely and refrigerate until you are ready to serve. Serve with tortilla chips or on top of Santa Fe Scrambler.

RED SALSA

Here is another great make-ahead salsa called *pico de gallo.*

SERVES 6

3 medium-size round tomatoes or 4 to 5 plum tomatoes (about 1½ pounds)

1 to 3 Serrano or jalapeño chiles

1 small white onion

10 to 12 sprigs cilantro

1 lime

1 teaspoon salt

Tortilla chips or Santa Fe Scrambler (see page 27), to serve

On your mark . . .

- Wash the tomatoes; cut out the stem circle at the top and discard.

- Cut the tomatoes in half, then cut each half into ¼-inch thick slices.

- Cut the slices into small chunks. Set aside in a medium-size bowl.

Get set . . .

- Slip on a pair of latex kitchen gloves. Remove the stems from the chiles and cut the chiles in half lengthwise. Rinse under cold water. Scrape out the seeds with the tip of a teaspoon and discard.

- Finely chop or mince the chiles and add to the tomatoes.

- Rinse the gloves and remove.

- Peel and finely chop the onion. Measure ½ cup and add to the tomatoes.

- Wash the cilantro, shake to remove excess water, and dry by rolling in paper towels.

- Gather the sprigs into a bunch and chop. Measure out ½ cup and add to the bowl.

- Cut the lime in half. Squeeze the juice into the tomato mixture.

- Add the salt.

- Mix the ingredients together and let rest at room temperature for about 1 hour.

Serve!

- Serve with tortilla chips or on top of Santa Fe Tofu Scrambler (see page 27).

GRITS AND CHEDDAR CHEESE SOUFFLÉ

This easy-to-make but glitzy soufflé comes from New Orleans. Grits are similar to a Native American corn dish, which makes them an authentic American food. If you live in the southern United States, you are familiar with grits and probably love them. But in the North, grits are under appreciated. So start a revolution in your neighborhood by cooking with grits.

SERVES 4 TO 6

5 tablespoons salted butter at room temperature

1 small white onion

2 scallions

4 large eggs

8 ounces cheddar cheese

1½ cups water

2 cups milk

1½ teaspoons salt

½ cup stone-ground grits

On your mark . . .

- Preheat the oven to 375°F with a rack in the middle slot of the oven.

- Butter a 2½-quart round casserole dish, or a soufflé dish, with 1 tablespoon butter.

- Peel and chop the onion into small dice. Measure out ¼ cup and set aside.

- Wash the scallions. Remove the stem end and any dark or discolored outer leaves. Cut into ¼-inch slices, measure out ½ cup, and set aside.

- To separate the egg whites and yolks, you will need one large and two small bowls.

- Holding one egg over a small bowl, crack the shell in two with a firm tap on the edge of the bowl. The white will spill out of the shell into the bowl. Pour the egg yolk back and forth between the two half shells, allowing the egg whites to continue to drop into the bowl. Drop the egg yolk into another small bowl. Add the separated egg whites into a larger, stainless steel, glass, or copper bowl (don't use plastic).

- Continue with the remaining eggs, following the same steps, until all the eggs are separated.

- Set the yolks and the egg whites aside.

- Grate the cheddar cheese on the largest holes of a four-sided grater. Measure 2 cups and set aside.

Get set . . . serve!

- In a small frying pan, melt 2 tablespoons of the butter over medium heat.

- Add the onion and sauté 3 to 5 minutes, until soft and translucent. Set the onion aside.

- Combine the water and milk in a saucepan and bring to a boil over high heat. Add the salt.

- Slowly pour in the grits and stir constantly with a whisk to keep the grits from developing lumps.

- Cook for 1 minute, still stirring to break up any lumps sticking to the side of the pan.

- Decrease the heat to low and simmer the grits for 15 minutes. Stir occasionally to prevent sticking.

- Remove from the heat and let cool for 3 to 4 minutes or until the grits are slightly thickened and firm to the touch.

- Add 1½ cups of the cheese, the egg yolks, sautéed onion, and the remaining 2 tablespoons of butter. Mix well.

- Beat the egg whites with an electric beater on high speed, or with a whisk, until just stiff, but not dry. You will know they are ready if the whites form peaks that hold their shape when you turn off the beaters and lift them out of the bowl.

- With a rubber spatula, fold about one third of the whites into the grits mixture to lighten it. Once they are blended in, fold in the remaining egg whites. There will be white steaks remaining in the mixture, but that is okay.

- Pour into the prepared baking dish and top with the remaining ¼ cup cheese.

- Place the soufflé on the middle rack of the oven and bake for 35 to 40 minutes, until the top is puffed and golden brown.

- The soufflé will deflate in size a bit after you remove it from the oven.

- Serve immediately.

CHEF'S TIPS

"Small dice" is a term that means using your knife to cut ¼-inch pieces of ingredients to ensure they cook faster.

It is important that you use a clean, dry bowl for beating your egg whites.

SNACKS AND CO-STARS

DEVILED EGGS

These heavenly deviled eggs are a sure crowd-pleaser, and they have a long American history. Washington Irving mentions "deviled dishes" in his famous tale, "The Legend of Sleepy Hollow." So, here is a tribute to old Washington (and Ichabod Crane, too) in my version of an American classic. Hard-boiled eggs can be difficult to peel, but if you follow this recipe, with a little patience, you will be able to peel the eggs perfectly.

MAKES 24

FILLING

½ cup mayonnaise, plus ½ teaspoon more if needed

½ teaspoon dry mustard

2 tablespoons unsalted butter at room temperature

2 teaspoons freshly squeezed lemon juice

2 to 3 dashes Tabasco sauce (optional)

1 dash Worcestershire sauce

1 teaspoon salt

½ teaspoon ground white pepper

EGGS

12 large eggs

1 teaspoon baking soda

4 to 6 cups ice cubes or more as needed

5 to 6 sprigs chopped flat-leaf parsley, to garnish

Paprika

On your mark . . .

- To make the filling, in a small bowl, mix together the mayonnaise, mustard, butter, lemon juice, Tabasco sauce, if using, Worcestershire sauce, salt, and white pepper until smooth. Cover and refrigerate while you prepare the hard-boiled eggs.

Get set . . .

- Put the eggs in a single layer in a non-aluminum saucepan. Carefully pour in water to 1 inch above the eggs. Add the baking soda to the water. Place the pan on top of the stove.

Cook!

- Bring the water to a boil, uncovered, over high heat.
- As soon as the water boils, turn off the heat. Cover and move the pan to a cold

burner to prevent further cooking. Let the eggs stand in the water for 17 minutes (use a timer so you don't forget).

- Place the pan with the eggs in the sink and gently fill it with cold water. Once the water is cold, add 4 cups of the ice to the pan.

- Let the eggs stand for 10 to 15 minutes in the ice water and then add the final 2 cups of ice. If all the ice melts, add more.

- To peel the eggs, gently tap off the tip of the shell.

- Hold the egg under a slow stream of cold water and gently peel away the shell. Place the peeled, whole egg in a clean bowl. Discard the shells. (They are great to add to your compost, though.)

- Remove the filling from the refrigerator and set it near the peeled eggs.

- Wet a sharp knife with cold water. Slice each egg in half lengthwise and remove the yolks. The tip of a butter knife works well for this. Place the yolks in the bowl with the filling. Lay the empty egg-white halves upside down on a paper towel to absorb any excess water. Repeat with the rest of the eggs. Place the egg whites right-side up on a clean plate.

- Using an electric hand-held beater, beat the filling and yolks until smooth. You can add an additional ½ teaspoon of mayonnaise if the filling is a little dry.

- To fill the egg white halves, you will need two teaspoons. Lift a spoonful of filling out of the bowl and use the other spoon to gently push it into the egg-white cavity. Repeat until all the shells are filled. Lightly cover the plate of finished deviled eggs with waxed paper or an aluminum foil tent. Refrigerate until you are ready to serve.

Serve!

- Wash the parsley, shake to remove excess water, and dry by rolling in paper towels. Finely chop and set aside.

- Arrange the eggs on a serving dish, sprinkle on chopped parsley and paprika, and serve cold.

CHEF'S TIP

Remember to cover and refrigerate any leftover deviled eggs or filling and eat within 3 days. The filling makes scrumptious egg-salad sandwiches.

YOGURT AND CUCUMBER DIP

Do you want something cool to eat when it is sizzling outside? The Greek dish *tzatziki* is the perfect way to chill on a hot day, but it is also a delicious small plate or appetizer any time of the year.

SERVES 4 TO 6

1 large cucumber

1½ teaspoons salt

2 cups Greek-style yogurt, or 1½ cups plain whole-milk yogurt

2 to 3 cloves garlic

5 to 6 sprigs mint

3 sprigs dill

3 tablespoons extra-virgin olive oil

1 tablespoon white wine vinegar

Freshly ground black pepper

Flatbread crackers or pita bread cut into triangles, to serve

On your mark . . .

- Wash and peel the cucumber.

- Using the largest holes on a four-sided grater, grate the cucumber into a large bowl.

- Add the salt and allow the cucumber to stand for 5 minutes.

- Put the grated cucumber into a hand-held strainer over the sink. With the back of a large spoon, press out the water and return the cucumber to the bowl.

Get set . . .

- Add the yogurt to the grated cucumber and mix well.

- Slightly crush the garlic by laying the flat side of a chef's knife on the clove and pressing firmly to break open the skin. Remove the skin, cut off the root end and discard. Mash the garlic with a fork until it is in small chunks. Scoop up the garlic and add it to the cucumber-and-yogurt mixture.

- Wash the mint, shake to remove excess water, and dry by rolling in paper towels.

- Wash the dill, shake to remove excess water, and dry by rolling in paper towels.

- Finely chop the mint and dill together, reserving a little of both for a garnish. Add the chopped herbs to the bowl with the cucumber-and-yogurt mixture.
- Add the olive oil, vinegar, and pepper and toss well to combine.
- Cover the dip and chill in the refrigerator for at least 30 minutes or overnight.

Serve!

- Add the garnish and serve cold with flatbread crackers or pita bread for dipping.

YOGURT, SOUR CREAM, & FETA CHEESE SPREAD

This little plate quickly satisfies guests who arrive at your house hungry and don't want to wait for the entree. Serve it as an appetizer, along with plenty of crusty bread or crispy sesame crackers.

SERVES 4 TO 6

½ cup of Greek-style yogurt, or plain whole-milk yogurt

¼ cup sour cream

1¼ cups crumbled feta cheese

3 tablespoons extra-virgin olive oil, plus more for drizzling

1 teaspoon dried oregano or thyme

2 ripe tomatoes

1 loaf crusty French or Italian bread or sesame crackers, to serve

On your mark . . .

- Combine the yogurt and sour cream in a medium bowl.
- Add the feta cheese, olive oil, and oregano.
- Using a hand-held electric mixer, blend on low speed for about 30 seconds, until smooth.

- Cover and chill the spread for at least 1 hour or overnight.

Get set . . .

- Wash the tomatoes; cut out the stem circle on top and discard. Chop the tomatoes into small chunks and place on top of the spread.

- Drizzle olive oil on top.

- Slice the bread, if using.

Serve!

- Serve the spread with the bread.

CHICK PEA AND GARLIC PUREE *Hummus*

You might be surprised to learn this very in-vogue spread is actually centuries old. Making it from scratch may seem like a lot of work, but the result is so tasty you'll forget the long preparation time. If you decide to make this dip from scratch, you'll need to start the day before in order to soak and cook the chick peas. You can also take a shortcut and use cooked, canned chick peas.

MAKES ABOUT 2½ CUPS

1 ⅓ cups dried chick peas (garbanzo beans) or 2 cups canned chick peas

3 cloves garlic

2 lemons

2 teaspoons salt, plus more as needed

1 cup Sesame Sauce (see page 47)

5 to 6 sprigs chopped fresh flat-leaf parsley

Flatbreads, crackers, or pita bread to serve

On your mark . . .

- Follow the package directions for cooking the chick peas, or if buying them in bulk, use the following cooking directions.

- Rinse the chick peas with cold water in a colander.

- Shake off any excess water and pour the beans in a single layer onto a clean tray. Carefully check for and discard anything that is not a chick pea, like a tiny stone.

- Put the chick peas in a 4-quart pot and cover with water. The water should cover the beans by 2 inches.

- Cover and refrigerate the chick peas for 8 hours or overnight.

- After they have soaked, skim off any skins that have floated to the surface and discard.

- Drain the chick peas in a large colander and rinse with cold water. Pour the drained beans into a large pot. Cover the chick peas with cold water and bring to a boil over high heat, then reduce to a simmer, partially covering the pot. Skim off any foam that rises to the top. Cook for 1 to 1 ½ hours or until tender. Reserve 1 cup of the cooking liquid, drain the chick peas in a colander, and they are ready to use.

■ If you are using canned chick peas, rinse under cold water, drain, and they are ready to use.

Get set . . .

■ Slightly crush the garlic by laying the flat side of a chef's knife on the clove and pressing firmly to break open the skin. Remove the skin, cut off the root end and discard.

■ Put the crushed garlic cloves in the bowl of a food processor with the chopping blade in place.

- Squeeze the juice from the lemons, remove any seeds, measure out ¼ cup and pour it directly into the bowl of the food processor.

- Add about ½ cup of the cooking liquid and 2 cups of chick peas to the bowl of the food processor. If using canned chick peas, add ½ cup cold water to the food processor. Add the salt.

- Lock the lid into place and with the processor running, add the sesame sauce (see page 47) in a slow, steady stream and process until the mixture is smooth.

- If the mixture seems a little dry, add a little more of the cooking liquid or cold water.

- Turn off the processor, open the lid, and taste for seasoning. Add a little extra salt or more lemon juice, as needed.

- Wash the parsley, shake to remove excess water, and dry by rolling in paper towels. Finely chop and set aside.

Serve!

- Spread the hummus evenly across a plate. Make a 2- or 3-inch indentation in the center of the hummus and fill it with the chopped parsley. Serve with flatbreads, crackers, or pita bread, or as a dip for fresh vegetables.

SESAME SAUCE

MAKES ABOUT 1½ CUPS

1 to 2 cloves garlic

1 cup tahini paste

1 cup cold water

1 teaspoon salt, plus more as needed

On your mark, get set . . . blend!

- Slightly crush the garlic by laying the flat side of a chef's knife on the clove and pressing firmly to break open the skin. Remove the skin, cut off the root end and discard.

- Put the crushed garlic cloves in the jar of a blender.

- Add the tahini paste, water, and salt.

- Press the lid firmly into place. Blend at high speed until the mixture is as smooth and thick as mayonnaise.

- Taste for seasoning. Add salt if needed.

- With a rubber spatula, scrape the sauce into a bowl or tightly covered glass jar.

- Cover and refrigerate until you are ready to use.

CHEF'S TIP

Sesame sauce will keep in the refrigerator in a tightly covered glass jar for up to 2 months.

RED BREAD

Crunchy, oil-rubbed slices of toasted bread with tomatoes, basil, and garlic are a familiar part of the American food scene even though the dish comes from Italy, where it is called *bruschetta*. Bread is one of the main ingredients in this recipe, so you will want to shop for just the right loaf. Crusty Italian bread, such as *ciabatta*, or a French bread, such as a *baguette*, will work best. Avoid plain white sliced bread. It is simply too boring for this celebrity appetizer.

SERVES 4

2 garlic cloves

2 to 3 ripe tomatoes or 10 to 12 cherry or grape tomatoes

5 to 6 fresh basil leaves

4 large slices bread, such as Italian *ciabatta*, peasant bread, French bread, or *baguette*

⅓ cup extra-virgin olive oil

Sea salt

Freshly ground black pepper

On your mark . . .

- Slightly crush the garlic by laying the flat side of a chef's knife on each clove and pressing firmly to break open the skin. Remove the skin, cut off the root end and discard.

- Wash the tomatoes; cut out the stem circle at the top, and discard. Chop the tomatoes into bite-size chunks. Place in a medium-size bowl and set aside.

- Wash the basil, shake to remove excess water, and dry the sprigs by rolling them in paper towels. Tear the basil leaves into small pieces and set aside.

Get set . . .

- Lay the bread slices on a baking sheet and toast under a broiler for 1 to 2 minutes on each side, until golden and crispy. Be careful not to burn them.

- Remove the slices. Rub one side with the garlic cloves.

Serve!

- On top of each slice, spoon the chopped tomatoes and basil. Drizzle with olive oil. Sprinkle on the sea salt and freshly ground black pepper to taste.

- Serve warm or cold.

TOMATO AND CHEESE LUNCH PIE

Here is an easy-to-make lunch pie similar to quiche, but without the fuss of making a separate crust. Any time you can find good tomatoes, you can enjoy the taste of summer with a slice of this pie. Picnic anyone?

SERVES 4

½ tablespoon salted butter

2 tablespoons plain dried bread crumbs

1 small onion

1 clove garlic

4 to 5 sprigs flat-leaf parsley

4 to 5 fresh basil leaves

2 large ripe tomatoes

1 tablespoon extra-virgin olive oil

4 large eggs

½ cup lightly packed freshly grated cheddar or Parmesan cheese

½ teaspoon salt

¼ teaspoon freshly ground black pepper

On your mark . . .

- Preheat the oven to 350°F with a rack in the middle slot of the oven.
- Using all the butter, grease the sides and bottom of a 10-inch cake pan.
- Sprinkle the bread crumbs over the bottom off the cake pan. Shake and tilt the pan back and forth until the bread crumbs cover the whole surface.
- Carefully tap out any excess crumbs and reserve.

Get set . . .

- Peel and finely chop the onion and set aside.
- Slightly crush the garlic by laying the flat side of a chef's knife on the clove and pressing firmly to break open the skin. Remove the skin, cut off the root end and discard. Chop garlic and set aside.
- Wash the parsley, shake to remove excess water, and dry by rolling in paper towels. Remove the stems and discard. Coarsely chop the leaves and set aside as well.

- Wash the basil leaves, shake to remove excess water, and dry by rolling in paper towels. Tear into small pieces and set aside.
- Wash the tomatoes; cut out the stem circle on the top and discard. Coarsely chop the tomatoes and set aside.

Cook!

- Heat a 10-inch skillet or cast-iron pan over medium-low heat. Add the olive oil and onion and garlic. Sauté for 5 to 6 minutes or until the onions become soft and translucent. Be careful not to burn them.
- Add the parsley and tomatoes and cook for another 5 minutes.
- In the meantime, break the eggs into a medium-size bowl and beat lightly. Add the grated cheese, basil, salt, and pepper to the beaten eggs. Set aside.
- Turn off the heat under the tomatoes. Set the cake pan next to the stove. Spoon the tomato mixture evenly across the bottom of the cake pan. Pour the beaten egg mixture over the tomatoes and sprinkle the reserved bread crumbs over the top.
- Bake on the middle rack of the oven for 30 to 35 minutes, until the crumbs are browned on top. Place the pie on a cooling rack for 10 minutes.
- To remove the pie from the pan, run a knife around the edge to loosen it from the sides.
- Place a serving dish that is larger than the baking pan on top.
- Using hot pads, turn the cake pan and serving dish upside down. The pie should slip out onto the serving dish. If not, repeat the steps above a second time. Cut into wedges and serve.

CELEBRITY SOUPS

TOMATO SOUP

Here it is . . . the original . . . the number one . . . THE soup! Is there anything more comforting than a cup of rich, velvety tomato soup? It is almost worth it to feel sick so you can eat this soup to feel better! How many times have you opened a can of a popular brand and thought, *Is this tomato soup?* Now you can make your own American classic and taste why this soup is such a stand-out among soup groupies.

SERVES 4

1 small red onion

1 small carrot

1 stalk celery

3 tablespoons unsalted butter

1 tablespoon extra-virgin olive oil

1 (28-ounce) can pureed Italian-style tomatoes

2 tablespoons whole-wheat flour

1 tablespoon tomato paste

1 tablespoon raw (turbinado) or granulated sugar

1 teaspoon salt

½ teaspoon freshly ground black pepper

2 cups tomato juice (not vegetable juice)

¼ cup heavy cream or whole milk (optional)

On your mark, get set . . .

- Peel the onion and chop into small chunks and set aside.

- Wash and peel the carrot. Slice the carrot into thin slices, finely chop, and add to the onion.

- Wash and finely chop the celery, including the leaves at the top, and add to the onion-and-carrot mixture. Set aside.

Cook!

- Melt the butter with oil in a 3- to 4-quart heavy-bottom pot over medium-low heat.

- Add the vegetable mixture and cook until the vegetables are translucent and tender. This will take about 5 minutes. Stir occasionally.

- Turn the heat to medium-high and add the flour all at once.

- Stir well to coat the vegetables and cook the flour. This will take 1 to 2 minutes. Continue to stir to prevent the vegetables from sticking. If the vegetables start to brown, lower the heat.

- Whisk in the tomatoes and stir well to prevent lumps.

- Add the tomato paste and stir until dissolved.

- Mix well to combine the tomato-and-vegetable mixture until smooth.

- Add the sugar, salt, and pepper.

- Cover the pan with the lid slightly ajar and lower the heat to simmer.

- Cook for 25 to 30 minutes or until the soup has thickened. Occasionally remove the lid and stir the soup to prevent sticking.

- Remove the pan from the burner and let the soup cool completely. This will take about 20 minutes.

- In the meantime, place a fine-mesh strainer over a large bowl and set aside.

- After the soup has cooled, ladle about half of it into the jar of a blender.

- Press the lid firmly in place and blend at high speed for about 30 seconds, or until smooth.

- Pour the soup into the strainer over the bowl.

- Blend the remaining soup in the blender with the lid pressed firmly in place at low speed for about 30 seconds.

- Pour the second batch of soup into the strainer with the first batch.

- Using the bowl of a ladle, press and stir the soup through the strainer to separate any solids from the soup. Discard the solids that remain in the strainer.

- Return the strained soup to the pan and add the tomato juice. Mix well to combine.

- Bring the soup to a simmer over low heat. This will take 10 to 15 minutes.

- When you are ready to serve, ladle the hot soup into four bowls. If you are using the milk or cream, add a little to each bowl.

- Serve hot.

BLACK BEAN SOUP

The black bean performs in high style in this simple but oh-so-good soup. Cooking dried beans takes a little effort, but afterwards you get to put those dark beauties to delicious use in this popular soup. If you don't have the time to make the soup from scratch, you can substitute a can of cooked black beans for the dried ones.

SERVES 4 TO 6

2 cups cooked black beans (see page 137) or 1 (15.5-ounce) can drained black beans

2 cups cold tap water, homemade Chicken Broth (see page 62), or canned low-sodium chicken broth

1 hard-boiled egg

1 small bunch cilantro

4 to 5 slices bacon (optional)

1 ½ teaspoons salt

On your mark, get set . . .

- Place 1 cup of the cooked beans in a blender. Add 1 cup of the water. Press the lid firmly into place.

- Blend on high speed for 2 to 3 seconds, until the beans have the consistency of thick cream. Some whole beans should remain.

- Pour the blended beans into a large saucepan.

- Pour the remaining cup of beans and remaining 1 cup water into the blender and blend at high speed for 30 seconds or until the consistency of thick cream. Add to the saucepan and set aside.

- Peel the hard-boiled egg, finely chop it, and set aside.

- Wash the cilantro, shake to remove excess water, and dry by rolling in paper towels. Coarsely chop and set aside.

Cook!

- If you are using the bacon, place the strips in a frying pan over medium-high heat and fry for about 3 minutes on each side or until just crispy.

- Remove the bacon from the pan, lay on paper towels to drain, and let cool.

- Cut the strips into small pieces and set aside.

- Set the saucepan with the soup over medium heat. Add the salt and bring the soup to a simmer, stirring frequently as it cooks. Using a metal spoon, skim off any foam or impurities that rise to the surface.

- Cook for 35 minutes at a gentle simmer.

- Serve hot and garnish with the chopped egg, cilantro, and bacon bits, if using.

CHEF'S TIPS

Look for canned black beans that are minimally processed and do not contain preservatives, or for vacuum-packed cooked beans.

Look for tips on hard-boiling eggs in the recipe for Deviled Eggs (see page 39).

CHICKEN BROTH

Homemade chicken broth not only tastes better than canned broth, it gives recipes an outstanding flavor. Why not take a little time and create your own? The finished stock will keep for up to 4 days in the refrigerator or for 3 months frozen.

MAKES ABOUT 2 QUARTS

3½ to 4 pounds chicken wings, necks, and thighs

2 medium onions

10 to 12 sprigs flat-leaf parsley

2 carrots

2 stalks celery

3 cloves garlic

10 black peppercorns

2 bay leaves

6 to 8 whole cloves

6 quarts cold water

On your mark . . .

- Put the chicken pieces in a colander and rinse thoroughly with cold water. Allow to drain as you prepare the rest of the ingredients.

Get set . . .

- Cut the onions in half without peeling them. Add to a pot large enough to hold all the ingredients.

- Wash the parsley, shake to remove excess water, and dry by rolling in paper towels. Coarsely chop and add to the pot.

- Scrub the carrots with a vegetable brush to remove any dirt, cut them into large chunks, and add them to the pot.

- Wash the celery, cut into large pieces, and add to the pot as well.

- Add the garlic cloves whole, with the skin, along with the peppercorns, bay leaves, and cloves.

Cook!

- Place the pan on the stove. Add the chicken and water.

- Bring the water to a boil over high heat. This will take about 25 to 30 minutes.

- Skim any foam or impurities that rise to the top.

- Once the stock boils, decrease the heat to a simmer, and cook for 2 hours.

- Continue to skim the stock as it cooks, about every 10 minutes. Turn off the heat and let the stock stand for about 10 minutes.

- Drain the stock through a fine-mesh sieve or colander into a heatproof bowl or pan.

- After the contents have cooled, separate the chicken meat from the skin and bones. Discard the skin and bones and the vegetables and reserve the chicken for another recipe, or a tasty sandwich.

- Cover and chill the stock in the refrigerator.

- Remove any fat that has hardened at the top and discard. The stock is now ready to use.

CHEF'S TIP

Always thaw frozen chicken stock overnight in the refrigerator or on the stovetop over medium heat. Never thaw it at room temperature.

STUYVESANT CORN AND POTATO CHOWDER

Fresh picked corn cut off the cob gets royal treatment in this classic chowder. The sweet corn that grows in and around Stuyvesant, a small agricultural community nestled along the Hudson River in upstate New York, is some of the best on the planet. A good friend who worked at one of the local farm markets asked me to come up with a recipe for chowder using local corn and potatoes. Just in case you can't get fresh picked corn, this recipe works perfectly with frozen.

SERVES 6 TO 8

8 ears fresh corn, or 4 cups frozen kernels

1 small yellow onion

5 small Yukon gold potatoes

4 slices thick-cut bacon, or 2 tablespoons salted butter

5 cups whole milk

4 tablespoons salted butter

2 teaspoons salt

½ teaspoon freshly ground black pepper, plus more if needed

1 to 2 jalapeño peppers

3 to 4 sprigs flat-leaf parsley, to garnish

On your mark . . .

- Husk the corn and remove the silk strands.
- Slice the kernels off the cob, reserving as much of the corn liquid as possible. To do this, stand the ear of corn on the stem end in a wide flat bowl or pan. Using a sharp knife, slice down in even rows to remove the kernels. Set the corn aside.
- Peel and chop the onion into small chunks and set aside.
- Wash and peel the potatoes, chop into small chunks and place in a medium-sized bowl. Cover with cold water and set aside.

Get set . . .

- If you are using the bacon, place the strips in a frying pan over medium-high heat and fry for about 3 minutes on each side or until just crispy.
- Remove the bacon from the pan, lay on paper towels to drain, and let cool.

- Cut the strips into small pieces and set aside.

- If you are not using the bacon, melt the butter over medium heat.

- Add the onions to the bacon fat or melted butter and sauté for 3 to 4 minutes over medium heat until soft and translucent. Using a metal slotted spoon, transfer the onions to a heatproof bowl and set aside.

- Drain the potatoes in a colander.

- Combine the onions and the potatoes in a 3- to 4-quart saucepan. Add enough cold water to just cover the potatoes.

- Bring the water to a boil over medium-high heat; do not cover the pan.

- Reduce to low and simmer the potatoes and onions for 15 minutes or until just tender, but not falling apart, when pierced with the tip of a sharp knife.

- Drain the potato and onion mixture and set aside.

Cook!

- In a 6- to -8 quart saucepan, combine the milk, corn, butter, potatoes and onions, chopped bacon, salt, and pepper.

- Bring to a gentle boil over medium-high heat.

- Reduce the heat to simmer and cook for 10 to 12 minutes or until heated through and simmering, stirring occasionally.

- While the soup cooks, slip on a pair of latex kitchen gloves. Remove the stems and cut the jalapeños in half lengthwise. Rinse under cold water. Scrape out the seeds with the tip of a teaspoon and discard. Chop into small dice and place in a small serving dish.

- Rinse the gloves and remove.

- Wash the parsley, shake to remove excess water, and dry by rolling in paper towels. Coarsely chop and put in a small bowl.

- Serve the chowder hot, and pass the jalapeños and parsley at the table to sprinkle on top.

NEW GAZPACHO WITH CHIPOTLE ALMOND CREAM

Gazpacho can be so exciting when the ingredients are fresh picked summer vegetables, including those treasured ripe tomatoes from your garden. But this gazpacho can even hold its head up high if made with supermarket vegetables in the middle of winter. The recipe calls for a blender to make the Chipotle Almond Cream but don't be tempted to make the soup in the blender. As you will see in the recipe, hand-chopping the vegetables takes a little more time, but it makes for soup with vivid color, fragrance, and amazing-in-your-mouth flavor and texture.

SERVES 6

GAZPACHO
2 ½ pounds fresh ripe tomatoes

2 red bell peppers

1 small red or Vidalia onion

1 small bunch of chives

1 cucumber

2 stalks celery

2 limes

1 small bunch cilantro

1 tablespoon salt

1 teaspoon freshly ground black pepper, plus more as needed

¼ cup extra-virgin olive oil

½ cup cold water

CHIPOTLE ALMOND CREAM
½ cup cold water

¼ cup extra-virgin olive oil

2 to 3 tablespoons finely chopped chipotle chiles in adobo sauce

1 clove peeled garlic

¾ cup slivered almonds

1 slice French bread, with crust removed, cut into small cubes

2 tablespoons balsamic or sherry vinegar

On your mark . . .

- First, make the gazpacho.

- Wash the tomatoes and cut out the stem circle at the top and discard. Chop the tomatoes, measure 3 cups, and add to a bowl large enough to hold all the ingredients.

- Wash the bell peppers. Cut in half and remove the seeds and veins. Chop into ¼-inch chunks and add to the bowl.

- Peel and chop the onion into ¼-inch chunks and add to the bowl.
- Wash the chives, shake to remove excess water, and dry by rolling them in paper towels. Chop the chives, measure ½ cup, and add to bowl.
- Wash the cucumber. Cut in half lengthwise and lay face down on the cutting board. Cut into long slices, about 1-inch thick. Stack the slices on top of one another. Cut the slices into ¼-inch chunks and add to the bowl.
- Wash the celery. Chop into ¼-inch chunks and add to the bowl.
- Cut the limes in half, squeeze the juice into a small bowl, and add to the bowl.
- Wash the cilantro, shake to remove excess water, and dry by rolling in paper towels. Coarsely chop the cilantro with the stems, measure out ½ cup, and add to the bowl. Save any leftover cilantro for another recipe.
- Add the salt, pepper, and olive oil.
- Gently combine all the ingredients with a large spoon. Taste the soup and add a little extra salt and pepper, as needed. Add the ½ cup of cold water, and cover the bowl. Set it to the side at room temperature for at least 1 hour, but no more than 3 hours.

Get set . . . serve!

- While the gazpacho stands at room temperature, make the chipotle cream.
- Combine the water, olive oil, chipotle chiles, garlic, almonds, bread cubes, and vinegar in the order written in the jar of a blender. Press the lid firmly in place. Blend at high speed for 10 to 15 seconds, or until just blended into a smooth paste.
- Scrape into a small bowl, cover with wax paper, and freeze for at least 1 hour or up to 3 hours.
- Chill the serving bowls for the gazpacho in the freezer or refrigerator for 1 hour or up to 3 hours.
- When you are ready to serve the soup, ladle it into the chilled bowls. Top with a tablespoon or so of the frozen chipotle almond cream.

STAR-STUDDED SALADS AND DRESSINGS

GREEN GODDESS DRESSING

This exotic dressing was invented at The Palace Hotel in San Francisco in 1923 to celebrate the opening night of a play called *The Green Goddess.* The head chef created the recipe to honor George Arliss, the play's star. The dressing certainly had star power! It became a salad-dressing legend; the play opened to rave reviews and was later made into a film that was nominated for an Academy Award. Over the years, the dressing has been modified, modernized, pasteurized, and homogenized. The version below recalls an American original in all its glory.

MAKES 1½ CUPS

1 cup mayonnaise

½ cup sour cream

3 tablespoons tarragon vinegar

3 scallions

3 anchovy fillets

1 bunch fresh chives

3 to 4 sprigs chervil or tarragon

4 to 5 sprigs flat-leaf parsley

1 lemon

½ teaspoon salt

½ teaspoon freshly ground black pepper

On your mark, get set . . . mix!

- In a large bowl, blend the mayonnaise and sour cream together with a whisk.

- Add the tarragon vinegar and mix until smooth.

- Trim the scallions and cut off the root end and discard. Finely chop the white bottoms and a few inches of green stems. Combine the scallions with the anchovies, chives, chervil, and parsley on a cutting board and finely chop. Add to the mayonnaise mixture.

- Using a whisk or a spoon, mix until combined into a thick paste. Squeeze the juice from the lemon, remove any seeds, and add the lemon juice, salt, and pepper to the bowl and mix well. Cover and refrigerate the dressing until you are ready to use.

CHEF'S TIP

Green Goddess Dressing will keep up to 1 week refrigerated in a tightly covered jar.

CHICKEN SALAD WITH GREEN GODDESS DRESSING

This Chicken Salad and Green Goddess dressing makes a glamorous co-star combo.

SERVES 6 TO 8

8 ounces bone-in chicken breasts with skin

8 ounces bone-in chicken thighs with skin

1 medium white onion

1 to 2 cloves garlic

1-inch-thick slice fresh ginger

8 to 10 sprigs flat-leaf parsley

5 whole black peppercorns

1 carrot

1 stalk celery

8 cups cold water

1 cup Green Goddess Dressing (see page 73)

Romaine or red or green leaf lettuce leaves, to serve

On your mark, get set . . .

- Rinse and pat dry the chicken pieces; place in a pot large enough to hold the chicken and vegetables.

- Peel and coarsely chop the onion and add to the chicken.

- Slightly crush the garlic by laying the flat side of a chef's knife on the clove and pressing firmly to break open the skin (no need to peel) and add to pot.

- Slightly crush the slice of ginger, skin on, with the flat side of a chef's knife and add to the pot as well.

- Wash the parsley, shake to remove excess water, and dry by rolling in paper towels. Coarsely chop 6 sprigs and add to the chicken. Refrigerate the remaining parsley for garnishing the finished salad.

- Add the peppercorns to the pot.

- Wash the carrot and celery, coarsely chop, and add to the pot.

Cook!

- Pour the water into the pot with the chicken and vegetables. Bring to a boil over high heat.

- Reduce the heat to simmer and cook for 30 to 35 minutes, until the chicken is cooked through and tender and the meat is no longer pink. As the liquid simmers, skim off any foam that rises to the top and discard.

- Let the chicken cool in the broth for 10 to 15 minutes or until the chicken is cool enough to handle.

- Lift the chicken out of the pot and put on a clean cutting board.

- Drain the cooking liquid through a strainer and discard the vegetables. Save the chicken broth for another recipe. It can be frozen.

- Remove the chicken skin and discard. Pull the meat from the bones and discard the bones.

- Cut the chicken into 1-inch cubes and put in a mixing bowl

- Coarsely chop the reserved parsley and add it to the chicken. Toss the parsley to coat the chicken cubes.

- Add the dressing to the chicken. Toss to coat the chicken pieces.

- Wash and pat dry the lettuce leaves and lay them on a serving platter. Top with the dressed salad.

- Serve immediately or chill until ready to serve.

SUMMER'S PICK MIXED GREEN SALAD WITH ITALIAN DRESSING

The salad bowl, filled with crunchy, snappy, colorful, summer-fresh ingredients tossed with a perfect dressing, has made cooks' reputations since the first head of lettuce came out of the garden. To make your salad reputation legendary, first find a farmers' market, farm stand, or even a local store that sells fresh salad greens. Even if you buy washed, bagged lettuce, make sure you wash the leaves thoroughly before using. This recipe gives you an Italian-style dressing, or you can use Green Goddess Dressing (see page 73).

SERVES 4 TO 6

1 small head romaine lettuce

1 small head Boston lettuce

½ bunch fresh spinach (about 6 ounces)

1 small head radicchio

½ red bell pepper

2 small carrots

2 stalks celery

2 ripe tomatoes

1 recipe Italian Dressing (see page 79)

Salt and freshly ground black pepper

On your mark . . .

- Fill a clean sink with fresh cold water.

- Tear off the leaves of the romaine and the Boston lettuce, the spinach, and the radicchio and drop them into the water. Let them soak for a few minutes, gently moving them around with your very clean hands to help dislodge any dirt.

- Lift the leaves out of the water and put into a colander to drain. Drain the water and clean any dirt or sand from the bottom of the sink.

- Refill the sink and repeat this step at least once more. Use a salad spinner to dry the salad greens. If you don't have a spinner, lay paper towels on a clean countertop and set the greens on top. Gently roll up the leaves in the paper towels to absorb the extra moisture. You may need to do this in two batches. You can refrigerate the greens rolled in the paper towels or use them immediately.

Get set . . .

- Wash the bell pepper. Remove the seeds and veins. Chop into small pieces and set aside.

- Wash and peel the carrots and cut them into thin slices.

- Wash the celery and cut into thin slices.

- Wash the tomatoes; cut out the stem circle at the top and discard. Cut the tomatoes into wedges.

- To assemble the salad, tear all the greens into bite-size pieces; do not cut them. Put the greens in a large serving bowl. Add the bell pepper, carrots, celery, and tomatoes. Toss well to combine. Cover with a clean damp cloth and chill until you are ready to serve.

Toss!

- When you are ready to serve the salad, remove the garlic clove from the dressing and discard.

- Close the jar and give it a shake. Pour the dressing over the salad. Add salt and pepper and toss well.

- Serve immediately.

CHEF'S TIP

Toss the salad with the dressing just before you serve it. That way it will be at its best—crisp, not soggy.

ITALIAN DRESSING

Versatile and delicious, this dressing can be used on salads, cold cooked meats, or as a dip for fresh-cut vegetables. It will keep refrigerated in a tightly sealed jar for up to a week.

MAKES ABOUT ¾ CUP

1 clove garlic

½ cup extra-virgin olive oil

1 tablespoon red wine vinegar

1 teaspoon salt

¼ teaspoon sugar

1 teaspoon freshly squeezed lemon juice

Freshly ground black pepper

On your mark, get set, shake!

- Slightly crush the garlic by laying the flat side of a chef's knife on the clove and pressing firmly to break open the skin. Remove the skin, cut off the root end and discard.

- Put the garlic in a glass jar with a lid. Add the olive oil, vinegar, salt, sugar, lemon juice, and pepper. Secure the lid on the jar and shake.

- Let the dressing stand for at least 10 minutes and up to 3 hours.

- When you are ready to serve, remove the garlic clove and discard. Cover and shake the jar just before pouring on the salad.

QUINOA AND BLACK BEAN SALAD WITH FRESH LIME DRESSING

Here is a sparkly salad that is not only beautiful to behold and simple to prepare, but also sure to create a sensation at your next party. It combines cooked quinoa, black beans, and a fresh lime dressing. Quinoa is a grain, and you may have walked right by it when shopping for rice. I like to think of it as the "new" brown rice, though there is nothing wrong with the old brown rice. Have you seen quinoa on a menu recently and were not quite sure what it was? You are about to discover what all the fuss is about. Make sure you buy rinsed quinoa for this recipe. Read more about quinoa on page 82.

SERVES 4 TO 6

1 cup rinsed quinoa

2 cups water

DRESSING

1 lime

3 tablespoons extra-virgin olive oil

1 teaspoon salt

½ teaspoon freshly ground black pepper

¼ cup sour cream

SALAD

2 medium Valencia or navel oranges

1 medium-size ripe tomato

5 to 6 sprigs cilantro

5 to 6 sprigs flat-leaf parsley

1 cup cooked black beans (see page 137) or canned

1 small cucumber

1 bunch fresh mint

½ cup chopped roasted, salted, cashews

On your mark . . .

- Place quinoa and water in a 1½-quart saucepan and bring to a boil. Reduce to a simmer, cover, and cook until all the water is absorbed (about 15 minutes). Let the quinoa cool to room temperature. Set the cooked quinoa aside.

- To make the dressing, squeeze the juice from the lime into a clean glass jar with a

"ANCIENT GRAIN RETURNS TO RAVES"

Quinoa (pronounced KEEN-WAA) dates back roughly 5,000 years to the Aztec and Inca farmers. The quinoa plant is rugged and can grow at very high altitudes. As it matures, it develops into a rainbow of colors from white, yellow, and pink to dark red, purple, and black. The plant can withstand extreme conditions and can grow up to 6½ feet tall. Technically not a grain, quinoa is a cousin to spinach, beets, and Swiss chard. It is prepared exactly like rice and has a mild, nutty flavor. NASA is testing it as a potential addition to the astronauts' menu on long-term space travels because of its near perfect combination of fiber, balanced amino acids, vitamins, minerals, iron, and protein. Quinoa grain can be made into biscuits, soups, tortilla, stews, and, as this recipe shows, enjoyed in salads when it is cooked. Make sure to buy rinsed quinoa. That means that the quinoa has been soaked to remove the bitter outer coating and is ready to cook.

lid. Add the olive oil, salt, pepper, and sour cream. Close the lid, shake well, and refrigerate until you are ready to serve.

Get set . . .

- Wash and peel the oranges. Remove as much of the white outer skin as you can. Cut the orange into ¼-inch slices. Set the slices aside.

- Wash the tomato; cut out the stem circle at the top and discard. Dice the tomato into small chunks and place in a large bowl.

- Wash the cilantro and parsley, shake to remove excess water, and dry by rolling in paper towels; coarsely chop.

- Add the quinoa, black beans, cilantro, and chopped parsley to the bowl with the tomatoes.

- Shake the dressing again and pour it over the ingredients in the bowl. Toss well to combine and set aside.

- Wash, peel, and slice the cucumber into thin slices.

Serve!

- Mound the tomato-quinoa-and-black-bean combination in the center of the serving platter.

- Arrange the orange slices and cucumbers around the edge of the platter.

- Wash the fresh mint, shake to remove excess water, and roll in paper towels to dry; remove the leaves from the stems and discard the stems.

- Garnish with the mint leaves and cashews.

- Serve immediately.

FRUIT SALAD WITH PINEAPPLE POPPY SEED DRESSING

What is really cool about a fresh fruit salad? It goes well with almost anything. You can serve it with pancakes, at picnics, or at parties on the patio. It also makes a tantalizing dessert.

SERVES 4 TO 6

DRESSING

2 Valencia or navel oranges

1 (1-inch-thick) slice fresh ginger

½ fresh pineapple or 2 cups, diced

2 tablespoons honey

2 tablespoons poppy seeds

¼ teaspoon ground cinnamon

FRUIT

2 cups mixed fresh berries (strawberries, blackberries, raspberries, or blueberries)

½ ripe cantaloupe

1 lime

2 apples

2 ripe kiwi fruits

1 medium-size ripe banana

On your mark . . .

- First prepare the dressing. Cut the oranges in half. Squeeze out the juice, remove any seeds, and add to the jar of a blender.

- Peel and mince the ginger slice and add to the blender.

- Using a sharp knife, cut off the outer skin of the pineapple and discard it. Cut out the tough core at the center and discard, as shown in the illustration. Cut the pineapple into bite-size chunks and add to the blender.

- Add the honey, poppy seeds, and cinnamon to the blender.

- Press the lid firmly into place and blend on high speed until smooth, about 30 seconds. Pour into a medium-size bowl and cover and refrigerate while you prepare the fruit.

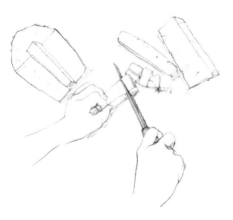

CUT THE PINEAPPLE

Get set . . .

- Wash the berries in a strainer. Shake off the excess water. If you have any strawberries in the mix, remove the stems from the tops and discard. Cut the strawberries into ¼-inch-thick slices.

- Put all the berries in a bowl large enough to hold all of the fruit.

- Scrape out and discard the seeds of the cantaloupe. Cut into slices. Cut the rind off the orange flesh and discard the rind. Cut the cantaloupe into chunks, measure out 2 cups, and add to the fruit in the bowl.

- Cut the lime in half and squeeze the juice into the fruit bowl. Toss well to combine.

- Wash the apples, cut into quarters, and remove the core and the seeds. Cut the apples into small chunks and add to the bowl. Toss well.

- Wash and peel the kiwis. Cut into ½-inch-thick slices and add to the bowl.

- Peel and slice the banana and add to the bowl.

- Pour the dressing over the fruit and mix well to evenly coat.

- Refrigerate for at least 1 hour and up to 4 hours, but not overnight.

Serve!

- Gently toss the fruit again to evenly distribute the dressing. Spoon into a serving bowl and serve immediately.

CHEF'S TIP

Shopping for fruit? Look for bright-colored skin, no dark spots, and a fragrance. If you are not sure if the fruit is ripe, ask for help in making your selection at the market or farm stand. Berries are picked ripe and will not ripen any further when you get them home. They should be refrigerated and used as soon as possible. Bananas will probably need to ripen when you get them to your kitchen.

SANDWICH AND BURGER SHOW STOPPERS

- - - - - - - - - - - - - - - - - -

NOT-AN-ORDINARY GRILLED CHEESE SANDWICH

MAKES 4 SANDWICHES

8 slices whole wheat, white, or sourdough sandwich bread

4 ounces sharp yellow cheddar cheese

3 tablespoons milk

3 tablespoons salted butter, melted

On your mark . . .

- Preheat the oven to 400°F with a rack in the upper slot of the oven.

Get set . . .

- Cut away the crusts of the bread with a sharp knife. Discard the crusts. Lay four slices on a small baking sheet.

- Using the largest holes of a four-sided grater, grate the cheddar cheese into a small bowl. Add the milk and combine.

- Butter the top of each slice of bread with a pastry brush. Turn the bread over so the buttered side is down.

- Spoon one-quarter of the cheese mixture on top of each slice of bread and cover with the remaining slices of bread.

- With a pastry brush, butter the top slices.

Cook!

- Place the baking sheet in the oven and bake the sandwiches for 10 to 15 minutes, until the cheese melts and the bread just begins to brown.

- Turn the oven to broil. Brown the sandwiches under the broiler for 1 minute on each side. (If necessary, reshape the sandwiches with a spatula after you turn them, tapping in the sides like a deck of cards.) Be careful not to let them burn.

- With a spatula, lift the finished sandwiches from the baking sheet to a serving dish. Let them cool for a moment, cut into halves, and serve hot.

PO-BOY SANDWICH: THE COMBINATION

Two brothers, Bennie and Clovis Martin, moved to New Orleans from Raceland, Louisiana, and became streetcar conductors. They eventually opened Martin's Coffee Stand and Restaurant in the French Market in 1922. The Martin brothers rocked the sandwich world forever when they came up with a stuffed 40-inch-long sandwich on a French roll. The startling new size was the right sandwich in the middle of the infamous 1929 street car strike, and 15 cents was the right price. The coffee stand was packed with locals buying the large sandwiches. Whenever one of the striking streetcar workers came up to the stand, Benny Martin would say, "Here comes another poor boy," and he would let them eat for free. The name stuck. If you consider that the hoagie probably didn't show up in Philadelphia until around 1936, and the hero followed soon after in New York, Po-boys were ahead of their time. Today, there is the grinder, wedge, bomber, torpedo, Italian sandwich, rocket, and the zeppelin. Call it what you will, it all started with the Po-boy.

MAKES 2 SERVINGS

1 small head lettuce

2 ripe tomatoes

12-inch French, Portuguese, or sub roll

1/4 cup mayonnaise

1/4 cup Creole mustard or whole-grain mustard

Tabasco sauce

8 ounces smoked ham, thinly sliced (not shaved)

4 ounces Swiss cheese, sliced

Sweet or dill pickle slices

On your mark . . .

- Preheat the oven to 350°F.

Get set . . .

- Remove any dark or discolored leaves from the outside of the head of lettuce. Cut the head of lettuce in half and wash under cold water. Tap the lettuce against the side of the sink to remove any excess water. Cut out the core and discard.

- Beginning at one end, slice the lettuce into very thin strips, the thinner the better.

- Place in a medium-size bowl and set aside.

- Wash the tomatoes; remove the stem circle from the top and discard. Cut the tomatoes into thin slices and set aside.

Assemble!

- Slice the French roll in half lengthwise, being careful not to cut all the way through the roll. It should fold open like a book.

- Place the roll on a baking sheet cut side up. Bake for about 10 minutes until the crust is crispy.

- Remove the roll and spread both halves with the mayonnaise and mustard.

- Add some dashes of Tabasco to each half, according to your taste.

- Layer the ham slices on one half of the roll.

- Layer the cheese slices on top.

- Layer the tomato slices on top.

- Layer the lettuce, then the pickle slices on top.

- Fold the top over to close.

- Cut the Po-boy in half or quarters and serve with plenty of paper napkins.

CHEF'S TIP

The perfect bread for a Po-boy should have a thin, crispy crust and a soft inside. Portuguese rolls will work very well or you can cut longer rolls down to 12 inches. Just cut off the ends to make the loaf uniform from end to end.

PULLED PORK SANDWICH

Who can resist mouth-watering, slow-cooked, pork barbecue on a roll? Cooking over a smoky, low fire introduces deep, savory layers of flavor to meats. The traditional 12 to 18 hours of careful tending that's required to achieve that legendary barbecue taste may not be available to everybody. Here is a roasted-in-the-oven pulled pork that is done in about 2½ hours, and it takes very little tending and generates no smoke.

SERVES 6

SPICE MIX

1 tablespoon smoked or regular paprika

1 tablespoon chile powder

2 teaspoons ground cayenne pepper

½ teaspoon ground coriander

2 tablespoons dark brown sugar

1 tablespoon salt

2 teaspoons freshly ground black pepper

THE PORK

1 tablespoon butter

3 pounds boneless pork butt or shoulder roast, trimmed of most of the excess fat

1 onion

2 cloves garlic

½ cup ketchup

½ cup homemade Chicken Broth (see page 62), canned low-sodium chicken broth, or water

2 tablespoons olive oil

6 plain hamburger buns

On your mark . . .

- To make the spice mix, combine the paprika, chile powder, cayenne, coriander, brown sugar, salt, and pepper in a small bowl and mix well.

- To prepare the pork, grease a heavy-bottom roasting pan, just large enough to hold the roast, with the butter.

- Rinse the pork roast with cold water and pat dry with paper towels or a clean kitchen towel.

- Lay the roast on a cutting board and rub the spice mix into the entire surface of the roast. Place the roast in the prepared pan.

- Immediately wash your hands with hot soapy water to remove any traces of the cayenne pepper.

- Tightly cover the pan with aluminum foil and let stand at room temperature for 30 minutes. Set a timer so you don't forget.
- Wash the cutting board with hot, soapy water. Dry the cutting board.

Get set . . .

- Preheat the oven to 325°F with a rack in the middle slot of the oven.
- Peel and cut the onion in half. Lay the two halves flat side down on a cutting board, cut into thin slices, and set aside
- Slightly crush the garlic by laying the flat side of a chef's knife on the clove and pressing firmly to break open the skin. Remove the skin, cut off the root end and discard. Coarsely chop and set aside.

Cook!

- Remove the foil from the roasting pan. Add the sliced onion and garlic to the pan.
- Combine the ketchup and chicken stock and pour into the bottom of the pan.
- Slowly pour the olive oil over the meat. Cover the pan tightly with the foil.
- Bake the pork on the middle rack of the oven for 2½ hours, or until the meat is very tender and easily falls apart and the tip of a sharp knife pierces the meat without resistance.
- Remove the pan from the oven and let the meat cool for 10 to 15 minutes with the foil cover on.
- Remove the foil and chop the roast into small chunks or shred the meat apart with two forks pulling in opposite directions.
- Return the pulled meat to the cooking liquid in the bottom of the pan and mix well to coat with the sauce.
- Slice open the buns and lay the bottom halves on a plate. Spoon on the pulled pork and pour some of the cooking liquid over the pork. Top with the other halves of the bun.
- Serve immediately.

THE BURGER
BURGER BASICS

- Buy freshly ground chuck or round steak.
- If you can, ask your butcher to twice grind the beef chuck or round steak. That second grinding will achieve the perfect texture.
- Once you get the meat home, refrigerate it until you are ready to cook.
- If you are buying from the meat section at a supermarket, purchase with the furthest expiration date from the day you buy it.
- Handle the meat as little as possible when forming the patties.
- If you have an exhaust fan in your kitchen, run it on high while you cook your burgers on the stove top or under the broiler. It will help remove cooking odors and smoke.

SERVES 4

1½ pounds ground chuck or ground round (80% lean) beef

2 tablespoons salted butter, melted

4 hamburger or kaiser rolls

SPICE MIX
1 teaspoon salt

¼ teaspoon cayenne pepper

½ teaspoon smoked or regular paprika

½ teaspoon freshly ground black pepper

FIXINGS
Romaine, iceberg, or Boston lettuce

Sliced red or white onion

Sliced sweet or dill pickles or sweet relish

Ketchup

Mustard

Mayonnaise

Tomatoes

On your mark . . .

- Wet your hands with cold water.
- On a clean cutting board, divide the beef into four equal portions.
- Lightly pat each portion into a patty 4 to 5 inches wide and ¾ of an inch thick. Try not to handle the beef too much. Overmixing it will cause the meat to lose its texture.

- With a spatula, lift the patties onto a clean plate

- Press your thumb in the center of the burgers to make a slight indentation. This will help the patties cook evenly. Cover with wax paper and refrigerate for 30 minutes and up to 2 hours.

Get set . . .

- To prepare the spice mix, combine the salt, cayenne, paprika, and black pepper in a small bowl. Add extra pepper, if you like. Set aside.

- Wash the lettuce leaves and shake off the excess water. Pat the leaves dry with paper towels. Tear the lettuce into pieces that will fit the hamburger buns and stack on a plate. Cover with wax paper and refrigerate until ready to serve the burgers.

- Peel and slice the onions into rings. Cover with wax paper and refrigerate until ready to serve.

- Place the fixings of your choice on a serving platter and cover and refrigerate until ready to serve.

- Wash, slice, and arrange the tomatoes on a serving dish, but don't refrigerate them.

Cook!

Under a broiler

- Dip a rolled sheet of clean paper towel into a little canola oil. Rub it onto the broiler pan rack to prevent the burger from sticking and to make washing easier.

- Turn on the broiler. Place the broiler pan under the broiler for about 2 minutes as it preheats. Set a timer so you don't forget.

- In the meantime, brush each burger with the melted butter on both sides and generously sprinkle the spice mix onto the top side.

- Place the burgers on the hot broiler pan. Close the oven door and broil for 4 minutes. For medium-well done, turn the burgers with a spatula and cook for another 5 minutes on the other side. For well-done, broil for 5 minutes on the first side, and 6 minutes on the other side. Remember to use a hot pad when handling

BAD BURGER-COOKING HABIT

While cooking, never press down on the burger with a spatula, no matter what cooking method you use. It does not reduce the cooking time, and it forces all the flavorful juices out of the meat.

the broiler pan.

On a stovetop

- Brush each burger with the melted butter on both sides and generously sprinkle the spice mix onto the top side.

- Use a skillet that is large enough to hold all the burgers. If necessary, use two skillets.

- Add any leftover butter to the skillet.

- Heat over medium-high heat until hot but not smoking. Carefully add the burgers and cook for 4 minutes. For medium-well done, turn the burgers with a spatula, and cook for another 5 minutes on the other side. For well-done, broil for 5 minutes on the first side, and 6 minutes on the other side.

On a grill

- Prepare the grill by using a barbeque brush to clean the grate. Take a paper towel dipped in canola oil and lightly rub the cold grill to coat it. It will help prevent the burgers from sticking. If using a gas grill, light it and follow the manufactures "direct cooking" method.

- If using charcoal, start the fire and wait until the coals have stopped flaming and are covered with a white ash.

- To prepare the burgers for cooking, brush both sides of the patties with the melted butter and sprinkle a generous amount of the spice mix onto the tops.

- Place the burgers directly over the coals or over the gas burners. Grill for 4 minutes. For medium-well done, turn the burgers with a spatula and grill for another 5 minutes on the other side. For well-done, grill for 5 minutes on the first side and 6 minutes on the other side. If your barbeque has a lid, keep it down while cooking the burgers.

- Serve the burgers hot on the buns and invite your guests to add whatever fixings they like.

FOOD SAFETY

The Food and Drug Administration says that thoroughly cooking the beef to a temperature of 160°F kills bacteria. Use an instant-read thermometer inserted into the center of the burger after it has cooked for the suggested time for an accurate temperature. Vary the cooking time according to temperature.

PIZZA COAST TO COAST

NEW YORK-STYLE PIZZA

Pizza may have been born in Italy, but it grew up in New York City. It all began in 1905 on Spring Street in Lower Manhattan. A young fellow named Gennaro Lombardi, a baker and *pizzaiolo,* had come to the United States when he was fourteen. He had the idea that if he baked the pizza he had loved in Naples, he might find folks who would crave it in New York City. So he had a coal-fired oven built in his store, jammed in some tables and a few chairs, and offered one item on the menu—a tomato and mozzarella pizza. It was love at first bite, and pizza madness was born in New York City. If you walk into any New York pizzeria today and say, "Can I get a slice?" you won't have to explain what that means. Its crust, sauce, and cheese only. You can also ask for a range of toppings, from anchovies to zucchini. The choice is yours. New York City is home to some of the best food in the world. And pizza probably is the dish that has the greatest following in The Big Apple. As any local will tell you, the pizza is only as good as the dough.

NEW YORK-STYLE PIZZA DOUGH

MAKES 1 12-INCH PIZZA

DOUGH
1½ cups warm water (100°F to 110°F)

1 (¼-ounce) package active Rapid-rise
   yeast

3 cups unbleached all-purpose flour,
   plus more for kneading

½ teaspoon salt

3 tablespoons extra-virgin olive oil

On your mark, get set . . .

In a food processor

- Carefully insert the all-purpose blade into the bowl of the food processor.

- Add the water, yeast, flour, salt, and olive oil to the food processor in that order. Close the lid and pulse the mixture until it comes together into a ball of dough. Turn off the processor. Carefully transfer the dough to a lightly oiled bowl. Give the ball of dough a few spins and turn it over to coat it with the oil. Now it is ready for a rest.

By hand

- Measure ¼ cup of the warm water into a small bowl.

- Sprinkle the yeast over the water, give the water a stir, and cover the bowl with plastic wrap.

- The water and yeast combination will need 10 minutes to become active. The yeast is active when soft bubbles appear on the surface of the water. If the bubbles do not appear, you'll have to start over with a new package of yeast and fresh water. Set the water and yeast combination aside.

- Pour the 3 cups flour into a large bowl and sprinkle the salt over the flour.

- With a spoon, make a well in the center of the flour.

- Combine the remaining 1¼ cups warm water and 2 tablespoons of olive oil in a measuring cup.

- Pour into the bowl with the flour, the water-and-yeast combination, and salt, and mix all the ingredients together. You should now have soft dough.

- Sprinkle a tablespoon of flour onto a clean work surface. Sprinkle extra flour on your hands to keep the dough from sticking to them. Pull the dough from the bowl and place it on the work surface.

- Begin kneading by pressing the dough away from you with the palms of your hands and folding it in half. Pick it up and give it a quarter turn to the right or left. Work the dough over and over for 5 to 6 minutes, repeating that same action. Be sure to keep turning the dough in the same direction. It will be sticky in the beginning, but don't worry.

- From time to time, give the dough a few punches to get the air out. Knead until it is smooth and springy. This will take about 7 to 10 minutes. Now it is ready for a rest.

- Drizzle the remaining 1 tablespoon of olive oil into a clean bowl and add the dough. Give the ball of dough a few spins and turn it over lightly to coat it with the oil.

KNEAD DOUGH

Rise!

- Cover the bowl with a sheet of plastic wrap and a couple of heavy, clean kitchen towels. Place the dough in a warm, draft-free spot, where it can rise undisturbed for 1 hour, or until it doubles in size.

- Now the dough is ready to be made into pizza or calzone.

NEW YORK-STYLE PIZZA PIE

SERVES 4

1½ cups canned chopped Italian-style
   tomatoes

8 ounces fresh mozzarella

3 tablespoons extra-virgin olive oil

2 teaspoons dried oregano

New York-Style Pizza Dough
   (see page 103)

Freshly ground black pepper

ADDITIONAL TOPPINGS

Pepperoni slices

Anchovy fillets

Fresh basil leaves pulled from the stem

Freshly grated Parmesan and/or Romano
   cheese

Pitted, sliced black olives

On your mark . . .

- Preheat the oven to 500°F with a rack in the middle slot of the oven.

- Lightly oil a 12- to 14-inch round pizza pan, a 10 ½ by 15 ½- inch baking pan, or a cookie sheet.

- Drain the tomatoes and shake off any excess liquid. Set aside.

- Using the largest holes of a four-sided grater, grate the mozzarella into a bowl. Add 1 tablespoon of the olive oil and toss. Set aside.

- Measure the oregano into a small bowl and set aside.

Get set . . .

- Place the dough on the baking sheet and, using your fingers and the palms of your hands, press and push the dough to stretch it to cover the pan.

- After the dough is stretched out to a thickness of about ¼ inch, use your fingers to make lot of tiny dents all across the surface.

- Brush the surface of the dough with the remaining 2 tablespoons olive oil.

- Top with the tomatoes, spreading them across the dough. Then sprinkle the mozzarella over the tomatoes. Sprinkle with the oregano and pepper.

- If you are using additional toppings, layer them on now.

Cook!

- Bake for 15 to 20 minutes on the middle rack, or until the crust is golden brown, crispy at the edges, and the top is bubbly. Slice and serve hot.

CALIFORNIA-STYLE PIZZA

The aroma of melting cheese and the subtle perfume of roasted garlic butter is irresistible in California pizza. This pizza is different from any other because it uses rye in the dough for texture and flavor. The dough begins with a spongy yeast starter that is then added to the flour. That technique is what gives the finished dough a very appealing chewiness and delicate taste. It all begins with outstanding dough. So here you go!

CALIFORNIA-STYLE PIZZA DOUGH

*MAKES DOUGH FOR 4 (4-INCH) INDIVIDUAL PIZZAS
OR 1 (14-INCH) PIZZA*

STARTER

⅓ cup rye or whole-wheat flour

1 (¼-ounce) package active Rapid-rise yeast

¼ cup warm water (100°F to 110°F)

¼ teaspoon sugar

DOUGH

1 tablespoon whole milk

¼ cup extra-virgin olive oil, plus extra for drizzling

½ cup warm water (100°F to 110°F)

1¾ cups unbleached all-purpose flour, plus extra for kneading

1 teaspoon salt

On your mark . . .

- To make the starter, put the rye flour in a large bowl. Sprinkle the yeast over the flour and add the water and sugar.

- Lightly mix the ingredients together with a spoon until they form thick dough.

- Cover the bowl with plastic wrap and place in a draft-free spot for 15 minutes.

Get set . . .

- To make the dough, combine the milk, ¼ cup of olive oil, and warm water in a small bowl.

- Combine the unbleached flour and salt in a medium bowl and whisk to mix.

CHEF'S TIP

Rapid-rise yeast is a type of instant yeast. Depending on the brand, it may be called Fast Rising, Rapid Rise, Quick Rise, and/or Bread Machine Yeast.

KNEAD DOUGH

- Add the milk mixture and flour mixture to the starter and mix together with a wooden spoon.

- Pull the dough out of the bowl onto a lightly floured cutting board or countertop. Lightly flour your hands, so the dough doesn't stick, and knead the dough for about 5 minutes, until smooth and spongy. Be careful not to use more than 2 tablespoons of flour to sprinkle on the work surface to prevent sticking. Continue to knead the dough by picking the dough up and giving it a quarter turn to the right or left. Keep turning and kneading the dough in the same direction. From time to time, give the dough a few punches to get the air out. Knead until it is smooth and springy.

- Drizzle a small amount of olive oil into a clean bowl and add the dough. Give it a couple of spins and then turn it over to lightly coat it with the oil.

Rise!

- Cover the bowl with a sheet of plastic wrap and a couple of heavy, clean kitchen towels. Place the dough in a warm, draft-free spot, and let it rise undisturbed for 50 minutes, or until it doubles in size.

- After the dough has finished rising, it is ready to bake into pizza. It can be used immediately or refrigerated for up to 4 hours. If you refrigerate the dough, keep it the bowl and cover it with plastic wrap.

- When you are ready to use the dough, bring it back to room temperature, covered with plastic wrap and a heavy kitchen towel. You can also freeze the well-wrapped dough. When you are ready to cook, thaw it overnight in the refrigerator. Bring it back to room temperature in a lightly oiled bowl that is covered with plastic wrap and clean kitchen towels.

CALIFORNIA-STYLE PIZZA WITH THREE CHEESES

MAKES 4 (4-INCH) INDIVIDUAL PIZZAS OR 1 (12-INCH) PIZZA

4 ounces mozzarella

3 tablespoons whole milk

4 ounces soft or fresh goat cheese

¼ cup freshly grated Parmesan cheese

1 bunch fresh basil

1 small bunch fresh chives

1 small bunch fresh arugula

1 ripe tomato

½ cup pitted black olives

¼ cup extra-virgin olive oil

California-Style Pizza Dough (see page 107)

2 tablespoons Roasted Garlic Butter (see page 125)

Freshly ground black pepper

Sea salt

On your mark . . .

- On the largest holes of a four-sided grater, grate the mozzarella into a medium-size bowl. Add the milk, the goat cheese, and the Parmesan cheese. Mix well to combine. Set aside.

- Wash the basil and shake to remove excess water. Pull the basil leaves off the stems and discard the stems. Measure ½ to ¾ cup of loosely packed basil leaves and lay them on a clean paper towel. Wrap the basil leaves in the towel to remove any excess moisture. Set the basil aside.

- Wash the chives, shake to remove excess water, and dry by rolling in paper towels. Coarsely chop the chives, measure out ¼ cup, and set aside.

- Wash the arugula in a large bowl of cold water. Let the leaves float in the water for a few minutes so that any dirt still clinging to them can fall to the bottom of the bowl. Lift the arugula up out of the water and transfer to a colander to drain. Wash and refill the bowl with cold water and repeat this step at least once. Drain the arugula a final time.

- Cut off and discard the arugula stems. Lay the arugula leaves on a few clean paper towels. Wrap the arugula leaves in the towels to remove any excess moisture. Coarsely chop the leaves, measure 1 cup loosely packed, and set aside.

- Wash the tomato; cut off the stem circle at the top and discard. Cut the tomato into small chunks and set aside in a small bowl.
- Chop the olives, add to the tomatoes, and toss well to combine. Set aside.

Get set . . .

To make one large pie

- Preheat the oven to 475°F with a rack in the middle slot of the oven.
- Pour about 1 tablespoon of the olive oil onto a 10 ½ by 15 ½ by 1-inch heavy aluminum or nonstick baking sheet and coat the bottom and sides evenly. Set the dough in the center of the tray, cover loosely with the plastic wrap, and let stand for 5 to 10 minutes.
- Using your fingers, spread the dough across the baking sheet until it is about ¼-inch thick. Gently press the dough into the sides of the pan to form a ridge.
- Brush the entire surface with olive oil, including the sides and top of the ridge.
- Using a large spoon or your fingers, carefully spread the garlic butter evenly across the surface but not the ridge of the dough
- Spread the arugula leaves evenly over the dough.
- Sprinkle the cheese mixture on top of the arugula.
- If the basil leaves are large, tear some of them in half. Lay them across the top of the arugula.
- Sprinkle on the chives.
- Top with the chopped tomato-and-olive combination.
- Drizzle the remainder of the olive oil across the surface of the pizza.

Cook!

- Bake for 15 to 20 minutes on the middle rack, until the pizza is browned and crispy.
- Remove the pizza from the oven and let it cool a few minutes.
- Gently slide a spatula under the pizza to loosen it, then carefully slide it onto a cutting board. Cut into slices with a sharp knife.
- Serve hot.

To make four individual pies

- Preheat the oven to 475°F with a rack in the middle slot of the oven.

- Cut the dough into equal sections and cover three of the sections with a clean cloth.

- Divide the garlic butter, cheese mixture, chives, arugula, and tomato-olive mixture into four equal parts.

- Using your fingers, spread one piece of the dough across the baking sheet until it is about ¼ inch thick and about 6 inches wide.

- Brush the surface of the dough with olive oil.

- Using a large spoon or your fingers, carefully spread one-quarter of the garlic butter evenly across the surface.

- Spread the one-quarter of the arugula leaves evenly across the dough.

- Sprinkle one-quarter of the cheese on top of the arugula.

- If the basil leaves are large, tear some of them in half. Lay one-quarter of the basil leaves on top of the cheese.

- Sprinkle on one-quarter of the chives.

- Top with one-quarter of the tomato-olive combination.

- Drizzle the olive oil across the surface of the pizza.

- Repeat this step until all four pizzas are formed.

Cook!

- Bake for 12 to 15 minutes on the middle rack, until the pizza is browned and crispy.

- Serve hot.

CHICAGO-STYLE PIZZA

A coast-to-coast selection of pizza in America is not complete without indulging in Chicago-style deep-dish pizza. The pie is thick-crusted and crispy, rich with olive oil, oozing with cheese, and fragrant with Italian sausage. Pizza-in-the-pan is an outstanding eating experience you won't soon forget. Some say it is the best in the country. Some say New York is best, and then there are those who swear California produces the best. The pizza wars rage on! Now you get to taste for yourself why those who love the pie from Chi-Town call it the answer to a pizza devotee's dream. Chicagoans love good pizza, and they demand the best. If you live in Chicago, you will think nothing of standing in line to get into your favorite pizza joint. Now you can make it at home. The dough for this pizza requires a 14-inch pizza pan that is 2 inches deep. You can substitute a cast-iron skillet or a baking sheet with 1-inch sides.

CHICAGO-STYLE PIZZA DOUGH

MAKES DOUGH FOR 1 (14-INCH) PIZZA

DOUGH

1 cup warm water (100° to 110°F)

2 (¼-ounce) packages active Rapid-rise yeast

1 tablespoon granulated sugar

3½ cups unbleached all-purpose flour

1 teaspoon salt

½ cup cornmeal

5 tablespoons extra-virgin olive oil plus more for drizzling

On your mark, get set...

In a food processor

- Carefully insert the all-purpose blade into the bowl of a food processor.

- Add the water, yeast, sugar, flour, salt, cornmeal, and olive oil to the bowl of the food processor in that order. Close the lid and pulse the mixture until it comes together into one ball of dough. Turn off the processor.

- Carefully transfer the dough to a lightly floured countertop or cutting board. Knead it a couple of times to make sure the dough is smooth. Now it is ready for a rest.

- Drizzle a small amount of olive oil into a large clean bowl and add the dough. Give the dough a few spins and turn it over to lightly coat it with the oil.

Rise!

- Cover the bowl with a sheet of plastic wrap and a couple of heavy, clean kitchen towels. Place the dough in a warm draft-free spot where it can rise undisturbed for about 1 hour, or until it doubles in size.

- Once the dough has risen, it is ready to bake into pizza.

By hand

- Measure ½ cup of the warm water into a small bowl.

- Sprinkle the package of yeast over the water and mix in the sugar. Give it a stir, then cover the bowl with wax paper or plastic wrap.

- The water-and-yeast combination will need 10 minutes to become active. The yeast is active when soft bubbles appear on the surface of the water. If the bubbles do not appear, you'll have to start over with a new package of yeast, sugar, and fresh water.

- Pour the flour into a large bowl. Add the salt and the cornmeal and mix well to blend the dry ingredients.

- With a spoon, make a well in the center of the flour. Add the yeast mixture, the 5 tablespoons of olive oil, and salt. Use a fork to mix the ingredients into a thick paste.

- Add the other ½ cup of warm water. Mix together until you have soft dough.

- Sprinkle a tablespoon of flour on a clean work surface. Sprinkle some extra on your hands to keep the dough from sticking to them. Pull the dough from the bowl and place it on the work surface. Divide the dough in half. Cover one half with a clean kitchen towel while you knead the other half.

- Begin kneading by pressing the dough away from you with the palms of your hands and then folding it in half. Pick it up and give it a quarter turn to the right or left. Work the dough over and over for 5 to 6 minutes, repeating the same action. Be sure to keep turning the dough in the same direction. It may be sticky when you begin, but don't worry.

- From time to time, give the dough a few punches to get the air out. Knead until it is smooth and springy. This will take about 7 to 10 minutes. Cover the dough. Knead the other half of the dough following the same steps. Combine both halves.

- Drizzle a small amount of olive oil into a clean bowl and add the dough. Give the dough a few spins and turn it over to lightly coat it with the oil.

KNEAD DOUGH

Rise!

- Cover the bowl with a sheet of plastic wrap and a couple of heavy, clean kitchen towels. Now it is ready for a rest.

- Place the dough in a warm, draft-free spot, where it can rise undisturbed for 1 to 1 ½ hours, until it doubles in size.

- Once the dough has fully risen, transfer it to a clean work surface. Give it a few punches to get the air out. Knead it for another 2 minutes. Now it is ready to bake into pizza.

CHEF'S TIPS

It is recommended that you make this dough in a food processor.

Rapid-rise yeast is a type of instant yeast. Depending on the brand, it may be called Fast Rising, Rapid Rise, Quick Rise, and/or Bread Machine Yeast.

CHICAGO-STYLE DEEP-DISH PIZZA

MAKES ONE 14-INCH PIZZA

1 (28-ounce) can whole Italian-style tomatoes

1 small bunch fresh basil (optional)

1 tablespoon dried oregano

1 teaspoon salt

½ teaspoon freshly ground black pepper

10 ounces mozzarella

8 ounces sweet Italian sausage

¼ cup extra-virgin olive oil

Chicago-Style Pizza Dough (see page 113)

½ cup freshly grated Parmesan cheese

On your mark . . .

- Thoroughly drain the tomatoes in a colander and discard the liquid. Pour the tomatoes into a large bowl and crush them into chunks with your very clean hands.

Get set . . .

- Preheat the oven to 475°F with one rack on the lowest slot and one rack in the middle slot of your oven.

- Wash the basil (if using), shake to remove excess water, and dry by rolling in paper towels. Remove the leaves and discard the stems. Tear the leaves in half, measure out ⅓ cup, and add to the tomatoes.

- Add the oregano, salt, and pepper to the bowl and mix well to combine. Set aside.

- Slice the mozzarella into thin slices and set aside.

- Remove the casings from the sausages by placing the sausages on a cutting board. With the tip of a knife, cut a slit in each casing the length of the sausage.

- Peel away the casings and discard. Using the flat side of the knife, spread the sausage meat across the surface of the cutting board. Chop the meat into small pieces. Set aside.

Cook!

- Pour 1 tablespoon of the oil into a 10-inch skillet over medium heat and heat until the oil is hot but not smoking.

- Add the sausage and sauté with a large slotted spoon for 4 to 5 minutes, breaking up the sausage as it cooks. The sausage is done when the meat is no longer pink. Remove the sausage from the skillet with the slotted spoon, put into a small bowl, and set aside.

- Use 1 tablespoon of the oil to coat the bottom and sides of a 14-inch pizza pan, skillet, or baking sheet. Lay the dough in the center. Cover with plastic wrap and let stand for 10 minutes.

- Using your fingers and the palms of your hands, spread the dough across the baking pan.

- Pull the edges of the dough up and then fold over to form a ridge all around the sides.

- Using the tines of a fork, prick the bottom of the dough at ½-inch intervals.

- Bake the dough on the lowest rack for 5 minutes. Set a timer so you don't forget.

- Remove the dough from the oven.

- Brush the entire surface, including the sides and the top of the ridge, with another tablespoon of the olive oil.

- Evenly cover the top of the dough inside the ridge with the slices of mozzarella.

- Evenly spoon the tomato mixture over the mozzarella.

- Sprinkle the grated Parmesan over the tomatoes.

- Evenly distribute the sausage pieces over the Parmesan.

- Lightly drizzle the remaining 1 tablespoon olive oil across the pizza.

- Return the pizza to the oven and bake on the middle rack for 30 to 35 minutes, or until the crust is lightly browned and crispy.

- To serve, slide the pizza out of the baking pan onto a cutting board. Cut into slices with a sharp knife and serve immediately.

DOUGH IN PAN

CALZONE

Waiting for calzone to cool when it first comes out of the oven takes some patience. But once you break it open and take that first bite, it's really worth it. If you're tempted to eat it with a fork, don't give in. It's portable pizza. Calzone means "trouser leg" in Italian and maybe that's why it gets around so much.

SERVES 4

8 ounces mozzarella

½ cup (4 ounces) ricotta cheese

½ cup (2 ounces) grated Parmesan cheese

1 teaspoon dried oregano

1 clove garlic

¼ cup canned Italian-style tomatoes with juice

2 ounces sliced pepperoni (about 1 cup) or sliced Genoa salami

New York-Style Pizza Dough (see page 103) or 1 store-bought pizza dough

3 tablespoons extra-virgin olive oil

4 to 5 fresh basil leaves (optional)

1 teaspoon salt

Freshly ground black pepper or red pepper flakes

On your mark . . .

- On the largest holes of a four-sided grater, grate the mozzarella into a large bowl.
- Add the ricotta, half of the Parmesan cheese, and ½ teaspoon of the dried oregano. Mix well and set aside.
- Slightly crush the garlic by laying the flat side of a chef's knife on the clove and pressing firmly to break open the skin. Remove the skin, cut off the root end and discard.
- Pour the canned tomatoes and garlic into the jar of a blender. Press the lid firmly into place. Blend at high speed for about 15 seconds , or until pureed.
- Pour into a small bowl and set aside.
- If you are using the salami, stack the slices into a couple of short piles. Cut each pile into strips about ½ inch wide. Set aside.

Get set . . .

- Preheat the oven to 500°F with a rack in the middle slot of the oven.

- Line a baking 10 ½ by 15 ½-inch sheet with parchment paper. You may have to fold the edges under to make the paper lay flat on the tray. Set the baking sheet aside.

- Lightly flour a cutting board or clean countertop.

- Sprinkle a little of the flour on the pizza dough to coat it. Cut the dough into four equal portions.

- Using your fingers and the palms of your hands, press each portion of the dough into a 6-inch circle.

- Brush the surface of the dough with some of the olive oil, leaving a 1-inch border without oil. Spread one-quarter of the cheese mixture on the bottom half of each of the dough circles, making sure to leave the 1-inch border clear of cheese.

- Add one-quarter of the pepperoni circles or salami strips to the bottom half of each circle. Tear the basil leaves in half and place them on top. Sprinkle ¼ teaspoon of the salt and pepper on each circle.

- Brush the 1-inch border of the dough with water where there is no filling.

- Pull the unfilled half of the dough over the filled half.

- Roll the edges of the dough together and press down with your fingers to seal. Using the tines of a fork, press the edges a second time to make an ever tighter seal. This extra step will keep the filling from leaking during baking.

- Carefully lift each calzone with your hands and place onto the prepared baking sheet.

- Brush the top with the olive oil.

- Brush each calzone with the tomato-and-garlic puree.

- Sprinkle the calzone with the remaining ½ teaspoon oregano and the remaining ¼ cup Parmesan cheese.

- Using a sharp knife, cut three short slits into each calzone. This will allow air to escape during baking.

CHEF'S TIP

Ready-made pizza dough may be purchased at a pizzeria or bakery. You can also find it frozen at your local supermarket.

Cook!

- Bake for 12 to 14 minutes on the middle rack or until the calzones are browned and lightly crisp.

- Remove the calzones from the baking sheet with a spatula and place on a cutting board. Cut into halves with a sharp knife.

- Serve hot.

SIDE SHOWS

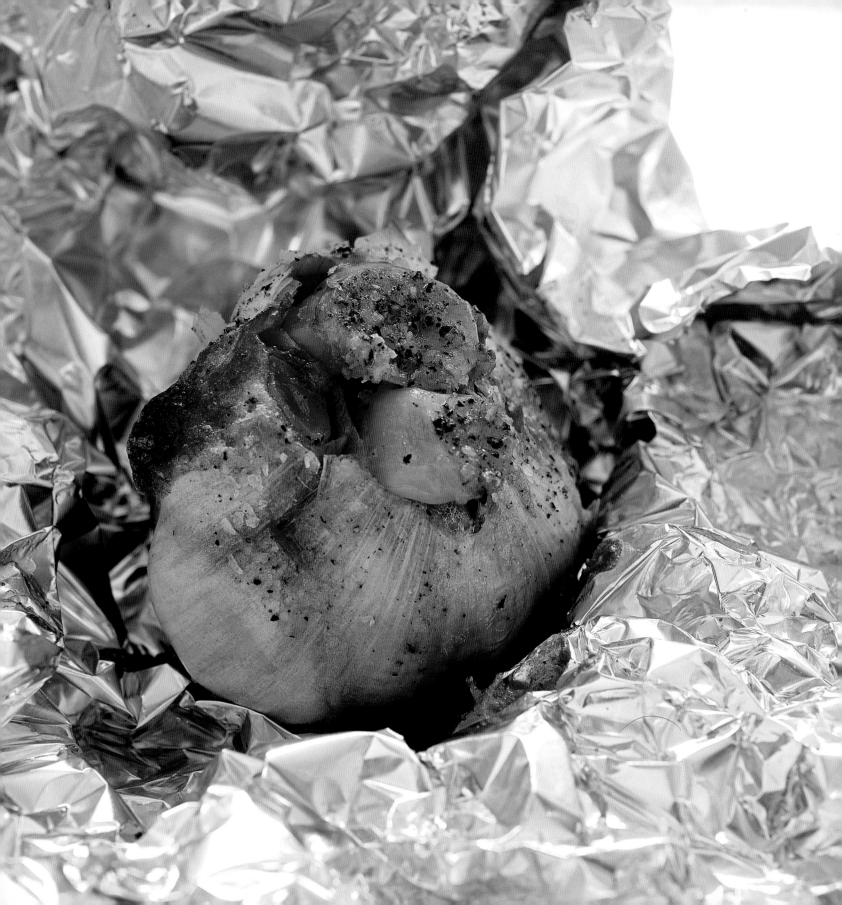

ROASTED GARLIC BUTTER

Garlic turns soft and silky when it's slow roasted. If the wallop of raw garlic is too much for you, why not roast it? The baked cloves can be squeezed out of their skins and blended into a savory butter, then placed in a jar and covered with extra-virgin olive oil to preserve the delicate flavor. Use it to spread like butter on bread, to make garlic-flavored mashed potatoes on page 131, or as a topping on California-Style Pizza on page 109. Say hello to garlic's mellow side.

MAKES ABOUT ½ CUP

4 heads garlic

⅓ cup extra-virgin olive oil

1 teaspoon kosher salt or coarse sea salt

1 teaspoon freshly ground black pepper

On your mark . . .

- Preheat the oven to 375°F with a rack in the middle slot of the oven.

- Remove the loose outer skin of the garlic heads by holding a head in your hands and gently rubbing off the dried outer skin. This is messy, so it's best to do it over a trash container.

- Cut about a 1½-inch slice off the pointed top of the garlic head to expose the raw cloves underneath. Discard the cut tops. When cutting off the tops, take care not to loosen the cloves from the head. Repeat with the other heads. It is not necessary to remove all the skin from the garlic heads.

Get set . . .

- Tear off four (12-inch) squares of aluminum foil.

- Set each head, cut side up, in the center of a piece of foil.

- Slowly pour 1 tablespoon olive oil over the garlic and allow it to sink into the cloves. Sprinkle on about ¼ teaspoon each of the salt and pepper. Set any extra to the side.

- Draw the foil up and around each head of garlic to make a roasting tent. Leave a small opening at the top for steam to escape.

- Place the tents on a small baking sheet.

CUTTING GARLIC

Cook!

- Bake for 45 minutes on the middle rack of the oven.

- Remove the baking sheet from the oven and gently pull down the foil to expose the garlic bulbs.

- Return the garlic to the oven and bake for another 15 minutes, or until cloves begin to brown and slightly pop out of their skins. Remove from the oven and let cool.

- Once the garlic is cool enough to handle, gently squeeze each clove from the bottom to extract the roasted clove. Set on a clean cutting board. Save any oil that is at the bottom of the foil tent and set aside.

- Repeat until all the cloves are removed from their skins and on the cutting board. This is a slow process, so be patient. Be careful to remove and discard all the garlic skins.

- With a fork, mash the cloves into a paste. Scoop up the paste and transfer it to a clean glass jar with a lid. Add the remaining salt and pepper and any oil in the bottom of the foil tents and mix well.

- Pour the remaining oil over the garlic paste and cover with the lid.

- Garlic butter will keep for 1 to 2 weeks in a tightly covered glass jar in the refrigerator.

QUICK-COOKED GREENS

Fresh greens retain their snappy color and delicious flavor when they are tossed together with a little oil in a skillet and quickly cooked. Collard greens, kale, and Swiss chard are packed with vitamins and nutrients, but in spite of that, it seems they don't get any respect! That is about to change when you try this recipe.

SERVES 4

1 pound collard greens, kale, green or red Swiss chard

2 tablespoons salted butter

1 tablespoon canola oil or peanut oil

1 teaspoon salt or to taste

On your mark, get set . . .

- Fill a clean sink with fresh cold water.

- Drop the greens into the water. Let them soak for a few minutes, gently moving them around with your very clean hands to help dislodge any dirt.

- Lift up the leaves and put into a colander. Drain the sink and clean any dirt or sand from the bottom.

- Refill the sink and repeat this step at least once more.

- Take one leaf at a time and lay it on a cutting board. Using the tip of a sharp knife, cut the stem out of the center of the leaf. Discard the stem or save to cook in another recipe. Stack the leaves in a separate pile. Continue until all the stems have been removed.

- Beginning at one end of the pile, tightly roll the leaves into a long cigar shape. Take your time doing this. If the pile is too big, divide it in half.

- After the leaves have been rolled, slice them crosswise into very thin strips, the thinner the better. This slicing technique is called *chiffonade*. Be patient, as this is a slow process.

- Once all the leaves have been cut into strips, gently toss them a few times to loosen them, and set them aside.

Cook!

- Melt the butter in a small pan and keep warm.

- Heat the oil in a 12- to 14-inch frying pan over medium-high heat for 30 seconds, or until the oil is hot but not smoking.

- Add the greens and salt.

- Sauté quickly until the greens have absorbed some of the oil and have turned a bright green.

- Continue to sauté for 2 to 3 minutes. Add the melted butter and toss to coat the greens.

- Serve immediately.

CHEF'S TIP

When shopping for kale, collards, or Swiss chard, pick the greens with the freshest, most brightly colored leaves, with no dark spots or shriveling.

MASHED POTATOES WITH ROASTED GARLIC BUTTER

Ptatoes mashed with Roasted Garlic Butter (see page 125), milk, and butter come together into a creamy delicate indulgence. What a concept! The abundance of potato varieties can be confusing. Here is a basic rule that applies: for baking and mashing, stick with Idaho or baking potatoes. When cooked, an Idaho potato has a light, floury texture that easily accommodates butter and milk.

SERVES 4 TO 6

2½ pounds Idaho, russet, or baking potatoes

1 tablespoon salt plus 1 teaspoon

4 quarts water

5 tablespoons salted butter

⅓ cup Roasted Garlic Butter (see page 125)

1 cup whole milk or half-and-half

On your mark . . .

- Peel and quarter the potatoes and drop them into large bowl of cold water to keep them from discoloring.

Get set . . .

- Bring the 4 quarts of water to a boil over high heat. Add 1 tablespoon of salt.

Cook!

- Drain the potatoes in a colander. Add them to the boiling water.

- The boiling water should just cover the potatoes. If not, add some additional hot water to cover the potatoes by 1 to 2 inches.

- Reduce the temperature to low and maintain a soft, low boil for 15 to 20 minutes, until the potatoes are tender and easily pierced with a fork.

- In the meantime, melt the butter in a saucepan. Add the garlic butter, remaining

1 teaspoon of salt, and milk. Heat over low heat until the butter is melted. Stir it into a smooth sauce. Turn the heat off and set aside.

- Drain the cooked potatoes in a colander. Return the drained potatoes to the pot in which they just cooked.

- Mash the potatoes with a wire masher.

- Fold the melted-butter-and-garlic sauce into the mashed potatoes with a wooden spoon until well combined.

- Serve immediately.

CRISP OVEN FRIES

Potatoes crisp up wonderfully when they are thin-sliced, given an herb coating, and baked in a hot oven. See if your guests can tell the fries weren't deep-fried when you serve them with The Burger (see page 97). Bet they can't.

SERVES 4 TO 6

4 medium-size Idaho, russet, or baking potatoes

5 tablespoons peanut or vegetable oil

¼ teaspoon dried oregano

¼ teaspoon dried sage

¼ teaspoon ground black pepper

½ teaspoon paprika

1 tablespoon course sea salt plus extra for flavor

On your mark . . .

- Wash and scrub the potatoes to remove any dirt.

- Cut the potato in half lengthwise and lay, cut side down, on a cutting board. Cut each half into 16 to 20 strips about ¼-inch thick. This is a slow process so take your time.

- Drop the cut strips into a bowl of hot tap water.

- Let the potatoes soak for 10 to 15 minutes.

Get set . . .

- Preheat the oven to 475°F with a rack in the middle slot of the oven.

- Coat a nonstick or heavy aluminum 10 ½ by 15 ½-inch baking sheet with 2 tablespoons of the oil.

- Mix the oregano, sage, pepper, paprika, and salt in a small bowl and set aside.

- Drain the potatoes.

- Lay two to three layers of paper towels on a clean work surface. Set the drained potatoes in batches on the paper towels. Wrap completely to dry. It is important to get the potatoes as dry as you can. The drier, the crispier.

- Put the potatoes in a large bowl. Pour the remaining 3 tablespoons oil over the potatoes and, with a spoon, toss well to coat. Sprinkle on the herb mix and toss again to evenly coat all the potatoes.

- Empty the potatoes onto the prepared baking sheet and spread them in a single layer. It is all right if some of them overlap.

Cook!

- Slide the baking sheet onto the middle rack of the oven.
- Bake for 25 to 30 minutes, until the potatoes are brown and crispy. Once or twice during the baking, open the oven and, using a spatula, loosen the potatoes. Use tongs to turn the loosened potato strips over to ensure even cooking. Turn the baking tray one full rotation during baking to prevent burning. If the potatoes start to burn, lower the oven temperature to 450°F.
- Remove the potatoes from the oven and sprinkle with extra salt.
- Serve immediately.

BLACK BEANS

Black beans, each one a jewel packed with protein, are naturally low in fat. Creamy and dreamy in a rich silky soup, served on a bed of fresh salad greens, in tacos, or as the ultimate side dish, black beans are a cook's best bud.

MAKES 4 CUPS

1 pound (2½ cups) dried black beans

8 cups cold water

1 small white onion

1 to 3 cloves garlic

2 tablespoons vegetable or peanut oil

2 teaspoons salt

On your mark . . .

- Rinse the beans with cold water in a colander.

- Shake off any excess water and arrange the beans in a single layer on a clean tray. Carefully check for and discard anything that is not a bean, like tiny stones or shriveled, very dark beans.

- Put the beans in a 4-quart pot and cover with the water. The water should cover the beans by 1 inch. Add more water as needed.

Get set . . .

- Peel and chop the onion and garlic into small chunks and add to the beans along with the vegetable oil.

Cook!

- Bring to a boil over medium-high heat.

- Partially cover the beans, reduce the heat to low, and cook at a gentle simmer for 1½ to 2 hours, until tender. Add hot water to the beans if the water level drops and exposes the beans. The hot water will allow the beans to cook uninterrupted.

- When the beans are tender, add the salt and cook for an additional 15 to 20 minutes.

- Turn off the heat. Drain the beans and serve hot, or allow them to cool completely. Refrigerate or freeze the beans until you are ready to use them.

SHOOTING STAR ENTREES

MAX MAC AND CHEESE

Macaroni and cheese, the most famous comfort food of all time (and the king of boxed meals) needs no introduction. Here is my cheesy valentine to Vermont, where cheese-makers produce more handmade, small batch, artisanal cheese than in any other state in the union. The recipe below is really simple, like-you-don't-even-have-to-cook-the-macaroni-first simple. Grating the cheese is the most time-consuming part of the recipe. I highly recommend that you grate it yourself! Not only will the cheese be freshly grated, you will also save a pretty penny per pound at the cheese counter. One more thing, Max Mac and Cheese might be the best macaroni and cheese you have ever tasted.

MAKES 6 SERVINGS

2 tablespoons salted butter

1 pound extra-sharp Vermont cheddar

8 ounces elbow macaroni

1¾ cups whole milk

¾ cup whole-milk cottage cheese

¼ cup light cream

1 teaspoon dry mustard

¼ teaspoon cayenne pepper

¼ teaspoon freshly grated nutmeg

½ teaspoon salt

¼ teaspoon freshly grated black pepper

On you mark . . .

- With a piece of wax paper, butter a 10-inch round baking dish with 1 tablespoon of the butter. Leave any leftover chunks of butter in the bottom of the baking dish.

- Using the largest holes of a four-sided grater, grate the cheese into a large bowl. You should have about 4 cups. You can also grate the cheese in a food processor. Follow the manufacturer's instructions for grating. Reserve ⅓ cup of the cheese in a small bowl and set aside.

- Pour the uncooked pasta into the large bowl of cheese and toss well with a spoon to combine the ingredients. Set aside.

Get set . . .

- Preheat the oven to 375°F with a rack in the upper third of the oven.

- Combine the milk, cottage cheese, cream, dry mustard, cayenne, nutmeg, salt, and pepper in the jar of a blender. Press the lid firmly in place and blend at high speed for 30 seconds.
- Remove the lid and pour the blended ingredients into the bowl with the cheese and uncooked macaroni. Toss thoroughly to evenly combine the cheese and macaroni.
- Pour into the prepared baking dish.
- Cover the baking dish with two layers of aluminum foil.

Cook!

- Bake for 30 minutes on a rack in the upper third of the oven.
- In the meantime, break the remaining 1 tablespoon butter into chunks and combine it with the reserved 1/3 cup grated cheese.
- After 30 minutes, remove the foil and sprinkle the cheese and butter combination across the top of the baking dish.
- Return to the oven, uncovered, and bake an additional 30 minutes, or until the top is browned and bubbly.
- Let cool for 15 minutes before serving.
- Cut into squares and serve hot.

OVEN-FRIED CHICKEN

Can you get juicy, crispy chicken without deep frying? Yes. The things that make Southern fried chicken so unforgettable—the crunch and the unmistakable flavor—are all here. What's not here are the 3 to 4 cups of oil used for frying. So next time you want a picnic feast of chicken, see why this hot-or-cold American favorite won't disappoint. Try serving this dish with Quick-Cooked Greens (page 127) and Mashed Potatoes with Roasted Garlic Butter (page 131).

SERVES 6 TO 8

2 cups buttermilk

2 tablespoons Dijon mustard

2 teaspoons salt

12 pieces skinless chicken thighs and skinless legs (about 3 ½ pounds)

2 cups Panko (Japanese-style bread crumbs) or plain dried bread crumbs

½ teaspoon dried sage

½ teaspoon freshly ground black pepper

1 teaspoon smoked or regular paprika

⅓ cup canola oil

On your mark . . .

- Combine the buttermilk, Dijon mustard, and 1 teaspoon of the salt in a large bowl.

- Add the chicken pieces and toss them well with a spoon to coat.

- Cover with wax paper and refrigerate for at least 1 hour, or overnight.

Get set . . .

- Preheat the oven to 425°F with a rack in the middle slot of the oven.

- Combine the bread crumbs with the remaining 1 teaspoon salt, sage, pepper, and paprika in a large bowl. Set aside.

- With a paper towel, lightly rub canola oil over the surface of a 13 by 9-inch baking rack and a 9 ½ by 13 ½-inch baking pan. This will make clean-up easier. Set the baking rack on top of the baking tray as shown in the illustration.

- Remove the chicken from the refrigerator.

BAKING PAN

- Roll the chicken pieces in the bread-crumb mixture to evenly coat each piece, shake off the excess, and lay the pieces on the baking rack. Do not crowd the chicken.

- Use a pastry brush to drizzle each piece with a little of the oil so you don't disturb the bread-crumb mixture.

Cook!

- Bake for 50 to 60 minutes, until the chicken is cooked through and golden brown, carefully turning the pieces over about halfway through the baking. Brush them with the remaining oil after turning. If some of the thigh pieces finish cooking before the legs, remove them to a warm platter and lightly cover with foil while the remaining pieces finish baking. To determine doneness, cut into one of the largest pieces to make sure there is no trace of pink inside. If the chicken is still pink on the inside, bake an additional 10 to 15 minutes.

- Serve hot or cold.

GLAZED PORK TENDERLOIN

The sauce for this elegant recipe is a sweet-and-savory combination of coconut and molasses. Surrounded by aromatic vegetables, the pork becomes juicy and tender with amazingly rich flavor. Serve it for a special occasion or when you want to show off just a little.

SERVES 4 TO 6

GLAZE

¼ cup molasses

¼ cup sweetened shredded coconut

¼ cup balsamic vinegar

2 tablespoon extra-virgin olive oil

1 teaspoon salt

¼ teaspoon cayenne pepper

PORK

2 (1¼-pound) pork tenderloins

1 tablespoon unbleached all-purpose flour

1 teaspoon salt

½ teaspoon freshly ground black pepper

1 medium carrot

1 clove garlic

1 small onion

1 stalk celery

2 tablespoons salted butter

½ cup ginger ale (not diet)

3 to 4 sprigs flat-leaf parsley

On your mark . . .

- To make the glaze, combine the molasses, coconut, vinegar, olive oil, salt, and cayenne pepper in a small bowl and mix until well blended. Set aside.

- To prepare the pork, with a sharp knife, remove any fat from the tenderloins.

- Combine the flour, salt, and pepper in a small bowl. Pour onto a sheet of 12-inch by 12-inch wax paper

- Roll the tenderloins in the flour mixture to evenly coat the outsides and lay them side by side in a baking dish.

- Brush the pork with about one-third of the glaze, cover with wax paper, and refrigerate for 20 minutes. Set a timer so you don't forget.

Get set . . .

- Wash and peel the carrot. Chop into medium-size chunks and add to a medium-size bowl.

- Slightly crush the garlic by laying the flat side of a chef's knife on the clove and pressing firmly to break open the skin. Remove the skin and root end and discard. Chop the garlic and add to the bowl with the carrot.

- Peel and chop the onion into small chunks and add to the bowl with the carrot and garlic.

- Wash the celery and chop into medium-size chunks, and add to the bowl with the other vegetables.

Cook!

- Preheat the oven to 400°F with a rack in the middle slot of the oven.

- Melt the butter over medium-high heat in an ovenproof skillet, large enough to hold both tenderloins. Make sure it has a lid.

- Add the pork to the pan and, using a pair of tongs to turn the tenderloins, brown on all sides. This will take 5 to 6 minutes. Remove the browned pork to a clean plate.

- Add the carrots, garlic, onion, and celery to the skillet and sauté for about 2 minutes or until the vegetables have begun to soften.

- Lay the pork on top of the vegetables and brush with another coating of the glaze. Pour the ginger ale into the bottom of the pan.

- Cover the pan and bake for 10 minutes.

- Brush the pork with another coating of the glaze and baste with any pan juices that have accumulated.

- Bake for 15 to 18 minutes, until an instant-read thermometer inserted into the thickest part of the tenderloin reads 145°F to 160°F.

- In the meantime, wash the parsley, shake to remove any excess moisture, and roll in paper towels to dry. Coarsely chop and set aside.

- Take the skillet out of the oven. Transfer the tenderloins to a warm platter and lightly cover with a sheet of foil.

- Place the skillet over medium-high heat, add any remaining glaze to the cooking liquid, and bring to a boil. Continue to boil, stirring to prevent sticking as the liquid reduces and slightly thickens. This will take 3 to 4 minutes. Remove the pan from the burner.

- Lay the pork on a cutting board and slice each tenderloin into 1-inch thick slices. Lay the slices on a serving platter and pour some of the cooking liquid and vegetables over the meat. Garnish with chopped parsley and serve hot.

FOOD SAFETY TIP

The Food and Drug Administration says that cooking pork to an internal temperature of 160°F safely kills bacteria. Most modern chefs, however, prefer to roast pork to 145°F (pink) to 155°F (medium), given how lean pork is today. Use an instant-read thermometer to get an accurate internal temperature. The choice of how much to cook the pork is yours.

CHICKEN POT PIE

Break through that flaky crust, see the chicken, and smell the aromatic vegetables and delicate sauce—and wonder if this is a special occasion, a holiday, or just the ultimate home-style dinner. Chicken pot pie might strike you as a little labor intensive because you have to make the crust. So if you'd rather make a quick pot pie, you can always stick a frozen one from the supermarket in the microwave. But if you want the real thing made from scratch, roll up your sleeves and dig one delicious, old-school dish that you won't soon forget.

SERVES 4 TO 6

PASTRY
1 cup unbleached all-purpose flour, plus extra for rolling the pastry

½ cup (1 stick) salted butter

3 ounces cream cheese (⅓ cup)

2 tablespoons ice water (optional)

FILLING
10 ounces boneless skinless chicken breasts

10 ounces boneless skinless chicken thighs

1 sprig thyme

1 sprig sage

5 to 6 sprigs flat-leaf parsley

1 medium carrot

1 stalk celery

1 medium white onion

5 cups cold water, plus more as needed

5 whole black peppercorns

1½ teaspoons salt

¼ cup (½ stick) salted butter

¼ cup unbleached all-purpose flour

½ cup light cream

1 cup frozen peas

On your mark . . .

- First, make the pastry.

In a food processor

- With the all-purpose blade in place, combine the flour and butter in the bowl of a food processor. Lock the lid and pulse 8 to 10 times, until the flour and the butter form a coarse mixture. Add the cream cheese and process until the dough just forms a ball. Add the ice water, 1 tablespoon at a time, as needed, to form the ball. Turn off the processor.

- Lightly flour a cutting board or clean countertop. Transfer the dough to the floured surface. Flatten the dough into an 8-inch round, about 1-inch thick. Sprinkle lightly with flour and wrap with plastic wrap. Refrigerate the dough while you prepare the filling ingredients.

By hand

- Pour the flour into a large bowl. Break the butter into chunks and add it and the cream cheese to the bowl. Using a pastry cutter, combine the ingredients until they form a coarse mixture. Add 1 tablespoon of the ice water and, using a wooden spoon, mix the dough together until it forms a ball. Add the second tablespoon of ice water, if needed.

- Lightly flour a cutting board or clean countertop. Transfer the dough to the floured surface. Flatten the dough into an 8-inch round, about 1-inch thick. Sprinkle lightly with flour and wrap with plastic wrap. Refrigerate the dough while you prepare the filling ingredients.

Get set . . .

- Rinse and pat dry the chicken pieces; place in a 4- to 6-quart heavy-bottomed pot.

- Pull the thyme leaves from the stems and discard the stems. Wash the parsley, shake to remove excess water, and dry by rolling in paper towels. Chop the sage leaves, thyme, and parsley together. Measure out about 2 tablespoons. Add 1 tablespoon of the chopped herbs to the pot with the chicken. Set the other tablespoon aside.

- Wash and peel the carrot. Wash the celery. Peel the onion. Coarsely chop the celery, carrot, and onion together. Add 1 cup of the chopped vegetables to the pot with the chicken. Set the remainder of the vegetables aside.

Cook!

- Pour the water into the pot with the chicken and vegetables. Add the peppercorns and salt. Bring to a boil over medium-high heat. Skim any foam that rises to the top and discard. If needed, add a little additional water to the pot to keep the chicken pieces covered as they cook.

- Once the water boils, reduce the heat to simmer, cover the pot with the lid slightly ajar, and cook for 30 minutes, stirring the chicken after 15 minutes to make sure it is submerged in the water and cooking evenly.

- Let the chicken cool in the chicken stock for 10 minutes.

- Using a slotted spoon, remove the chicken pieces to a clean cutting board.

- Pour the contents of the pot through a mesh strainer set over a large heatproof bowl or saucepan. Discard the solids in the strainer. Reserve 2 cups of chicken stock for the pot pie. Cool and refrigerate or freeze the remainder for another recipe.

- Pour the reserved stock into a medium-size saucepan, bring to a boil over high heat, then reduce the heat to simmer.

- Meanwhile, when the chicken is cool enough to handle, pull it apart into strips, place in a bowl, and set aside.

- Preheat the oven to 425°F with a rack in the middle slot of the oven.

- Heat a 2-quart saucepan over medium-high heat and add the butter. Be careful not to let the butter brown. If it does, reduce the heat. Once the butter is hot and melted, add the flour all at once and stir with a whisk or wooden spoon into a thick paste called a *roux*. Cook for 1 to 2 minutes, stirring constantly to prevent sticking.

- Add the reserved 1 cup chopped vegetables and reserved 1 tablespoon herbs to the roux. Cook for 2 to 3 minutes, stirring constantly until the vegetables are evenly coated.

- Add the cream and stir until smooth.

- Gradually ladle in about 1 cup of the simmering chicken stock and stir until it is smooth. Add another ladle of simmering stock and stir until smooth. Continue adding the rest of the stock until the sauce is smooth and thickened. Cook for about 1 minute, stirring frequently, to prevent sticking.

- Add the shredded chicken and bring the sauce to a simmer over medium heat. Cook for another 1 to 2 minutes, stirring carefully, until the chicken is coated with the sauce.

- Remove from the heat and let the filling cool for 15 minutes. Add the frozen peas to the cooled chicken filling and lightly toss with a spoon to combine.

- Remove the pastry from the refrigerator. Lightly flour a clean countertop. Sprinkle some flour on a rolling pin.

- Spoon the filling into a 10-inch pie dish, ovenproof skillet, or round baking dish.

- Lightly dust the pastry with some flour. Roll the pastry into a round that is large enough to cover the filling, leaving about a 2-inch overlap. Lay the pastry over the chicken filling. Roll up the overhanging edges to create a ridge all around the pie. Using the tines of a fork, gently press the pastry into the edges of the pie dish to seal it. Make a couple of slits in the center of the dough to allow steam to escape during baking.

- Place the pie on the middle rack of the oven and bake for 30 minutes, or until the crust is golden brown.

- Let the pie cool for 15 minutes.

- Use a large spoon to scoop up equal amounts of filling and crust and serve hot.

SEAL WITH FORK

SPAGHETTI AND MEATBALLS WITH FRESH TOMATO SAUCE

This dish is light and fresh tasting because no canned tomatoes or tomato paste are used and because the meatballs are not fried. You can prepare this in summer when garden-fresh tomatoes are abundant but also during the rest of the year when only supermarket tomatoes are available. It is faster to prepare than you might think, once you assemble the ingredients.

SERVES 4

MEATBALLS

8 ounces (2 links) sweet or hot Italian sausage

5 to 6 sprigs flat-leaf parsley

1 yellow onion

8 ounces ground beef

1 large egg

¼ cup dried plain bread crumbs

¼ cup freshly grated Parmesan cheese

¼ teaspoon ground freshly grated nutmeg

½ teaspoon salt

½ teaspoon crushed red pepper flakes

1 tablespoon extra-virgin olive oil

SAUCE

2 pounds (about 8) ripe plum tomatoes

1 small bunch basil

2 cloves garlic

1 small yellow onion

¼ cup extra-virgin olive oil

1 teaspoon dried oregano

1 teaspoon salt

1 teaspoon sugar

1 teaspoon freshly ground black pepper

2 cups homemade Chicken Broth (see page 62) or canned low-sodium chicken broth

PASTA

12 ounces spaghetti

2 teaspoons salt

Freshly grated Parmesan cheese, to serve

On your mark...

- To make the meatballs, remove the outer casing of the sausage by making a slit down the outside of the link with the tip of a sharp knife. Peel away the casing and discard.

- Wash the parsley, shake to remove excess water, and dry by rolling in paper towels. Separate the leaves and discard the stems. Coarsely chop the parsley and measure ¼ cup firmly packed.

- Peel and finely chop the onion. Measure 1 tablespoon and set aside the rest for another recipe.

- With the all-purpose chopping blade in place, combine the sausage meat with the ground beef, parsley, onion, egg, bread crumbs, Parmesan cheese, nutmeg, salt, red pepper flakes, and olive oil in the bowl of a food processor. Snap the lid into place.

- Pulse the food processor on and off 15 times, until the ingredients are well mixed.

- Remove the meatball mixture, being careful of the blade, and put it into a medium-size bowl. Scoop up a generous tablespoon of the meat mixture, shape it into a ball, and lay on a clean plate. Continue to form another 15 meatballs. Cover with wax paper and refrigerate.

Get set...

- To prepare the sauce, wash the tomatoes, cut off the stem circle at the top and discard.

- Chop the tomatoes into medium-size chunks, measure out 4 cups, and place in a large bowl. Gently squeeze the tomatoes with your very clean hands to break them down into a soupy liquid. Set the tomatoes aside. Wash your hands.

- Wash the basil to remove any sand or dirt, shake to remove excess water, and dry by rolling in paper towels. Remove the leaves from the stems, tear the leaves into small pieces, and set aside. Discard the stems.

- Slightly crush the garlic by laying the flat side of chef's knife on the clove and pressing firmly to break open the skin. Remove the skin, cut off the root end and discard. Chop the garlic and set aside. Peel and chop the onion medium-fine and set aside.

Cook!

- Heat the olive oil in a 4-quart sauce pan for 30 seconds over medium-high heat until hot but not smoking. Add the garlic and onion, and sauté for 3 minutes or until translucent. Add the tomatoes, basil, oregano, salt, sugar, black pepper, and 1 cup of the chicken broth. Bring to a boil, cover the pan with a lid slightly ajar, and cook for 5 minutes. Stir occasionally to prevent sticking. Skim and discard any foam that rises to the surface.

- After 5 minutes, reduce the heat to low, and using a pair of tongs, carefully add the meatballs to the sauce one at a time.

- Once you have added all the meatballs, add the final cup of chicken broth to the sauce and stir gently to combine the ingredients. Cover the pan with the lid slightly ajar, reduce the heat to simmer, and cook for 15 minutes or until the meatballs are firm and cooked through. The meatballs are done when you slice one open and it is no longer pink on the inside.

- In the meantime, bring 3 to 4 quarts of cold water in a large pot to a boil over high heat. Add the salt.

- Cook the pasta according to the package directions until *al dente*. Put the grated cheese in a serving bowl and set aside. Drain the pasta in a colander and pour it into a large serving bowl. Pour the sauce over the pasta and toss well.

- Serve hot. Offer the grated Parmesan cheese to your guests in a separate bowl.

CHEF'S TIPS

If you don't have a food processor, no problem. Just follow the directions for removing the sausage casing, then chop the meat into small chunks and combine it in a large bowl with the rest of the meatball ingredients. Mix well with a spoon or your very clean hands. Wash your hands.

Al dente means "to the tooth." The pasta retains a slightly hard center when you bite it.

ALABAMA FESTIVAL SHRIMP

Fresh lime and orange juices dress grilled shrimp up in a totally delicious way that is so good that you'll want to make it again and again. Shrimp is America's favorite seafood. In fact there's even a National Shrimp Festival in the heart of Gulf Shores, Alabama. It draws an estimated 300,000 shrimp lovers each year to feast on thousands of pounds of fresh-caught Gulf of Mexico shrimp. Here is an adaptation of one very popular recipe from the festival. Once you try it, you will see why visitors stand in line to taste it. You will need bamboo or metal skewers for the shrimp.

SERVES 4

SHRIMP
24 large, fresh shell-on shrimp (16/18 count per pound)

MARINADE
1 lime
1 orange
2 tablespoons honey
1 tablespoon Dijon mustard
1 clove garlic

4 to 5 fresh basil leaves, or 1 teaspoon dried
2 sprigs thyme, or 1 teaspoon dried
2 to 3 sprigs flat-leaf parsley
⅓ cup extra-virgin olive oil, plus extra for greasing
1 teaspoon salt
Freshly ground black pepper

On your mark . . .

- Clean and devein the shrimp. To do this, peel the shrimp and discard the shells. Take one shrimp and lay it flat on a cutting board. Using a paring knife, make a slight cut in the outside curve of the shrimp. You will find a black vein. Remove it by pulling it out while rinsing the shrimp under cold water. Repeat with the rest of the shrimp.

- Skewer a shrimp by passing the tip of a bamboo or metal skewer into the thickest part. Make the shape of a tight "C" by then passing the tip of the skewer through the tail. Pull the shrimp to the bottom of the skewer and continue with the next five shrimp. Lay the skewer on a non-aluminum tray. Repeat with the rest of the shrimp.

■ Cover the shrimp with wax paper and place in the refrigerator.

SKEWERED SHRIMP

Get set . . .

■ Wash the lime and the orange and dry them.

■ Using a potato peeler, peel off three slices each of the outer skin of the lime and the orange, being careful not to cut too deeply into the skin. Stack the slices on top of each other and cut them into thin strips. Mince the strips into small dice, measure out 2 tablespoons, and put in the jar of a blender.

■ Squeeze the juice from the orange, remove and discard any seeds, and pour the juice into the jar of a blender. Cut the lime in half, squeeze out the juice, and add to the blender.

■ Add the honey and Dijon mustard.

■ Slightly crush the garlic by laying the flat side of a chef's knife on the clove and pressing firmly to break open the skin. Remove the skin, cut off the root end and discard. Chop the garlic coarsely and add it to the blender.

■ Wash the basil and parsley, shake off any excess moisture, and dry by rolling in paper towels.

■ Coarsely chop the basil, thyme, and parsley and add to the blender. If using dried herbs, add them now.

■ Add the olive oil, then salt and pepper to taste.

■ Blend at high speed for 30 seconds, or until smooth.

■ Remove the shrimp from the refrigerator and pour the marinade over them. Turn over each skewer so that the marinade evenly covers the shrimp.

■ Refrigerate for 45 minutes or up to 90 minutes. Set a timer so you don't forget.

■ Remove the skewered shrimp to a clean platter, cover with foil, and refrigerate. Reserve the marinade.

Cook!

- Pour the reserved marinade into a small saucepan and bring to boil over medium heat. Boil for 1 minute, reduce to a simmer, and cook for 5 minutes. Stir occasionally to prevent sticking.

Under a broiler

- Lightly oil a broiler pan rack. Set the broiler to high and place the pan underneath it to heat for 1 to 2 minutes.

- Lay the skewers of shrimp on the broiler pan rack. Broil for 3 to 4 minutes on each side. Turn the skewers with a pair of tongs. Cook until the shrimp are lightly browned and firm to the touch.

- Remove the finished shrimp from the skewer and lay them on a serving platter, pour on some of the cooked marinade, and serve hot. You can also leave the shrimp on the skewer for each guest to remove.

CHEF'S TIP

It is important to bring the marinade to a boil and then simmer for 5 minutes as a food safety precaution, because the marinade was in contact with raw shrimp.

FONDUE PARTY

Do you fondue? It is easy to do, and the best part is that your guests get to do their own cooking. You just have to prepare and assemble all the ingredients and then settle down for a cozy, social get-together with friends and family where sharing a good meal is the most important part. Fondue cooking has been around for more than one hundred years. It made its way to the United States in the mid 1950s, and it is as popular today as ever. You could say, "Everything old is fondue again!" Here are basic tips, suggested dipping ingredients, and two popular recipes to get you started.

There are several types of fondue pots to choose from, including electric, gel- or alcohol- fueled, candle, or range-top pots. For dessert fondues, candle-powered fondue pots work just fine. But you will need an electric, gel- or alcohol-fueled pot to successfully achieve the temperature needed to keep cheese fondue creamy and cook meats, fish, or vegetables. Make sure you purchase a set that has long forks with color-coded, fireproof handles. That way everyone can choose a color and keep a close eye on his or her fork while the food cooks. Most importantly, read the directions that come with your new fondue set.

FONDUE ETIQUETTE

- Once you dip your fork, with its piece of bread, fruit, or cake, into a fondue pot, let it drip into the pot for a few seconds before you pull it away.

- Provide your guests with a dinner fork at each place setting so the fondue morsel can be slipped off the dipping fork, dipped into sauces, and your guest can eat the morsel without worrying about getting burned.

- When dipping, cover your bread with enough cheese the first time and skip the need to double dip.

- Never use your fingers. Ouch!

- Move your fork with its morsel in a figure 8 as you dip. It keeps the fondue mixture smooth and prevents lumping.

- There are traditional fondue rules that say if you lose your forkful of food in the pot, you have to kiss everyone at the table. That is up to you!

- The golden crust that forms at the bottom of the cheese fondue pot is delicious and can be scraped up and shared with your guests.

CHEESE, PLEASE, FONDUE

This recipe is a favorite and championed by fondue lovers. What is it about a creamy, warm, cheesy sauce swirled around a crusty bite of bread that is so irresistibly delicious?

SERVES 4

8 ounces Emmentaler cheese

4 ounces Gruyère cheese

8 ounces smoked Gouda cheese

2 tablespoons arrowroot or cornstarch

1/2 teaspoon salt

1/4 teaspoon freshly grated black pepper

1/4 teaspoon freshly grated nutmeg

2 cups buttermilk

1 clove garlic, peeled

DIPPERS

Assorted cubes of Italian, French, whole-wheat bread with crust still on

Pita bread cut into small wedge

Bite-size pieces cooked chicken or ham cubes

Bite-size raw broccoli, sweet red peppers or asparagus spears

Apple slices

On your mark, get set . . .

- Grate the cheeses on the largest holes of a four-sided grater into a large bowl. Sprinkle on the arrowroot or cornstarch, salt, pepper, and nutmeg. Toss together to evenly mix and set aside.

- Prepare your breads by cutting them into bite-size cubes. Prepare your vegetable and fruit by cutting them into bite-size chunks or slices as well. Cover your dippers with wax paper until ready to serve.

Cook!

- Heat the buttermilk and garlic in a heavy-bottomed pan over low heat on the stove top. Bring to a gentle simmer.

- Remove the garlic.

- Add the cheese mixture, a few handfuls at a time, stirring constantly. Add the next handful after the previous one has melted. Stir constantly until all the cheese mixture has been added and the fondue is smooth.

- Transfer to a fondue server. Ignite the fuel source and let it heat gently for a few minutes to make sure it is hot.

- Invite your guests to place the dippers of their choice on their fondue forks and dip away.

RED-CARPET DESSERTS

CHOCOLATE FONDUE

What is the most luxurious dessert you can make without a lot of work? How about a fragrant chocolate fondue along with an assortment of fresh fruits, cakes, cookies, and sweet bread cubes, all ready for the lucky dippers around your table.

SERVES 4

FRUIT DIPPERS (Prepare about 1½ cups of dippers for each guest.)

Sliced apples, pears

Seedless grapes, raspberries, and/or strawberries

Peeled and sliced bananas, kiwi fruit, and/or pineapple

Oranges

1 lemon or lime

Soft cookie chunks, cake chunks, and/or cinnamon bread cubes

Marshmallows

CHOCOLATE SAUCE

½ cup heavy cream

12 ounces Toblerone chocolate bars (or pick your favorite brand)

1 tablespoon whole milk (optional)

On your mark, get set . . .

- Wash the apples and pears and cut into slices. Wash the grapes and berries. Peel and cut the banana into slices. Peel and cut the kiwi, pineapple, and oranges into slices or bite-size chunks. Read more about cutting pineapple on page 83.

- Arrange the fruit on a serving platter and squeeze the lemon or lime over it, to prevent it from darkening.

- Arrange the soft cookie chunks, cake chunks, and/or cinnamon bread cubes on another serving platter.

- Cover the dippers with wax paper until you are ready to serve.

Cook!

- Pour the cream into a medium-size saucepan and heat gently over medium heat.

- Break the chocolate into chunks and add to the cream. Stir until melted.

- Add the milk if the melted chocolate is too thick, and blend together to thin.

- Pour the sauce into the fondue pot and place over a candle burner. Invite your guests to select from the platters and dip.

CARROT LAYER CAKE

Just looking at this moist and elegant carrot cake explains why it has so many fans. If you have never made a frosted layer cake, start with the recipe below. You can make your job even easier by baking the cake in a 9 by 13-inch pan, then all you have to do is frost the top. This cake will impress everyone who tries it, but most of all you!

MAKES 1 (9-INCH) TWO-LAYER CAKE, OR 1 (9 BY 13-INCH) CAKE

SERVES 8

CAKE

1 teaspoon unsalted butter

7 to 8 carrots (about 1 pound)

2½ cups unbleached all-purpose flour

1 teaspoon baking powder

1 teaspoon baking soda

¼ teaspoon ground cinnamon

¼ freshly grated nutmeg

½ teaspoon salt

½ cup canola oil

1½ cups raw (turbinado) sugar

1 cup whole-milk yogurt

¼ cup heavy cream

4 large eggs

2 teaspoons pure vanilla extract

½ cup chopped walnuts or pecans

CREAM CHEESE FROSTING

11 ounces cream cheese

½ cup shredded sweetened coconut

1½ cups confectioners' sugar

1 tablespoon freshly squeezed lemon juice

CHEF'S TIP

If you like a large amount of frosting on your cake, the frosting recipe may be doubled.

On your mark . . .

- Preheat the oven to 350°F with a rack in the middle slot of the oven.

- Lay two 1-foot sheets of parchment paper on top of one another on a clean countertop. Using the bottom of a 9-inch cake pan, trace a circle on the top piece of paper. Using the pencil line as a guide, cut out two layered circles. Set the circles aside.

- With a piece of wax paper, butter two round 9-inch cake pans with 1 teaspoon butter. Sprinkle on 1 teaspoon flour, tip the pans back and forth, and roll the pans on their sides to evenly coat the surfaces. Tap out any excess flour. Line the bottom of each pan with a parchment circle and set aside.

Get set . . .

- To make the cake, wash and peel the carrots. Using the largest holes of a four-sided grater, grate the carrots into a large bowl (or grate the carrots using a food processor. Follow the manufacturer's directions for grating.) Measure 3 cups grated carrots. Set aside.

- With a whisk, combine the flour, baking powder, baking soda, cinnamon, nutmeg, and salt in a bowl. Set aside.

- In the bowl of a food processor with the all-purpose metal blade in place, combine the carrots, oil, and raw sugar. Snap the lid into place and process for 20 to 30 seconds, until the ingredients are blended and smooth.

- Pour the mixture into a large bowl. Add the yogurt, cream, eggs, vanilla, and nuts. Beat the mixture with an electric hand-mixer set on high until the ingredients are blended into a smooth batter.

- Using a spatula, scrape the batter into the flour mixture and fold to combine until the ingredients come together. Don't over mix.

- Using a rubber spatula, scrape half of the batter into each prepared cake pan.

Cook!

- Bake on the middle rack of the oven for 30 minutes. The cake is done when a knife inserted in the middle comes out clean.

- In the meantime, make the frosting. Combine the cream cheese, coconut, confectioners' sugar, and lemon juice in a large bowl. Mix the ingredients with an electric hand-mixer until smooth. Cover and refrigerate until you are ready to frost the cake.

- Set the cake pans on a cooling rack and let cool for 5 minutes. Run a knife around the inside edge of the pan to loosen the cake.

- Lay a cooling rack on top of a cake pan and invert it. Carefully lift off the pan and the parchment paper. Now lay a second cooling rack on the cake and turn it upside down so the top of the cake is facing up. Repeat with the other cake pan. Cool the cake layers completely before frosting.

- To frost the cake, lay one layer on a serving dish, round side up. Using a long, thin metal or rubber spatula or a knife, put about ½ cup of the frosting in the center of the bottom layer. Spread the frosting to the edges of the layer until even. Take your time to avoid tearing the cake.

■ Lay the second layer on top of the first, round side up, making sure the layers evenly line up. Frost the top layer of the cake with another ½ cup of the frosting. Frost the sides of the cake with the remaining frosting, filling in with frosting where the two layers meet.

■ Cut into slices and serve.

OATMEAL RAISIN COOKIES

Oh, the oatmeal cookie. What an inspired creation . . . a portable bite of bliss. There are very few things that can match the irresistible aroma of cookies baking. And somehow, no matter where you are, this aroma will find you. Homemade is always worth the effort—especially with cookies. I recommend that you bake these cookies one baking sheet at a time to make sure they cook evenly.

MAKES ABOUT 3 DOZEN COOKIES

1 cup unbleached all-purpose flour

½ cup whole wheat flour

2 cups old-fashioned rolled oats (not instant)

1¼ cups raw (turbinado) sugar

½ teaspoon baking soda

1 teaspoon ground cinnamon

¼ teaspoon freshly grated ground nutmeg

½ teaspoon salt

1 cup (2 sticks) unsalted butter, at room temperature, plus ½ teapoon for greasing

¼ cup whole milk

2 tablespoons molasses

1 large egg

1 teaspoon pure vanilla extract

¾ cup chopped walnuts

½ cup raisins

On your mark

- Preheat the oven to 350°F with a rack in the middle slot of the oven.

- Using a piece of wax paper, lightly grease two 10 ½ by 15 ½-inch cookie sheets with ½ teaspoon butter. Set aside.

Get set . . .

- Combine the all-purpose and whole-wheat flours, oats, raw sugar, baking soda, cinnamon, nutmeg, and salt in a large bowl. Whisk until well mixed.

- In a separate bowl, combine the butter, milk, molasses, egg, and vanilla.

- Beat with an electric hand-mixer at medium speed until the mixture is smooth. Add to the dry ingredients. Toss all of the ingredients together to moisten.

- Mix in the nuts and raisins.

Cook!

- Scoop up about a tablespoon of dough and drop onto the greased cookie sheet. Repeat until you have 12 cookies about 2 inches apart.

- Bake one sheet at a time on the middle rack of the oven for 18 minutes, or until the edges are crisp and start to color. Let the cookies cool on the baking sheet for 10 minutes.

- In the meantime, prepare and bake the next tray. Continue until all the cookies are baked.

- Once the cookies have cooled for 10 minutes, use a spatula to lift them off the cookie sheet and place them on a rack to cool completely.

PLAYLAND ICE CREAM SANDWICH

Once upon a time there was an amusement park on the shore of the Pacific Ocean in San Francisco. The rides had names like Kookie Kube, Kiddie Bulgy, Loop the Loop, Rocketship, Shoot the Chute, and The Whip. There was even The Diving Bell, which took riders 30 feet underwater to get a glimpse of fish swimming—including real sharks and octopuses. Playland at the Beach is gone, but this famous frozen treat has survived. Back then, you could only get it at Playland. Now you can make a great version of it in your kitchen. You just have to provide the roller coaster rides.

MAKES 4

8 Oatmeal Raisin Cookies
  (see page 175)

About ½ cup vanilla ice cream

¾ cup Ghirardelli 60% cacao
  bittersweet chocolate chips

On your mark, get set . . .

- Line a small baking sheet with wax paper or parchment paper.

- Let the vanilla ice cream stand at room temperature for 10 minutes to soften.

- Lay four of the cookies on the baking sheet.

- Add a scoop, about 2 tablespoons, of the slightly softened vanilla ice cream on top of each cookie. Top with the second cookie to make a sandwich.

- Press down gently to bring the ice cream to the edge of the cookies. Smooth the edges of the ice cream with a knife.

- Repeat with the remaining the cookies until you have four sandwiches.

- Freeze for 30 minutes.

Cook!

- You will need to make a double boiler. To do this, take a medium-size saucepan and place it on the stove. Add 1 cup of water to the pan. Bring the water to a simmer over low heat. Do not boil.

- In the meantime, remove the sandwiches from the freezer and place them on a sheet of wax or parchment paper.

- Place a stainless steel bowl or a pot that is large enough so that the bottom of the bowl does not touch the simmering water. Add the chocolate and stir constantly until melted. Immediately turn off the heat and, using a pot holder, remove the bowl from the pan. Make sure you don't get any water into the melted chocolate, or it will be unusable.

- Spoon about 1½ tablespoons of the melted chocolate over each sandwich top and let the soft chocolate drip down the sides.

- Return the sandwiches to the freezer for 30 minutes.

- Serve immediately or if you want to serve later, wrap each sandwich in a couple of squares of wax paper. Return to the freezer until you are ready to serve.

CHEF'S TIP

If you can't find Ghirardelli chocolate, look for chocolate that contains at least 60% cacao to ensure that the melted chocolate will evenly coat the cookies. Use baking chips, not baking squares or chocolate bars.

CHOCOLATE CHIP COOKIES

This cookie hall-of-famer might never have happened if the inventor had done her shopping a bit more carefully. The scene is The Toll House Inn, Whitman, Massachusetts, which is about to run out of its popular cookie, the Butter Drop Do. The owner, Ruth Wakefield, gets set to bake a batch. She quickly discovers the kitchen is out of Baker's chocolate. Yikes! She decides to substitute some broken-up chips of semisweet chocolate, figuring it will melt into the dough as the cookies bake. But when the cookies come out of the oven, Ruth takes one look and knows they are no Drop Do. Maybe she didn't realize it at that moment, but she had just invented what would become the most famous cookie in the world. Cookie freaks are forever grateful to that chip snafu that took place one lucky morning in Whitman, Massachusetts.

MAKES 24 COOKIES

2¼ cups unbleached all-purpose flour

1 teaspoon baking soda

1 teaspoon salt

½ cup (1 stick) unsalted butter

¼ cup chunky peanut butter

1½ cups raw (turbinado) sugar

2 large eggs, slightly beaten

1 teaspoon pure vanilla extract

12 ounces (2 cups) semisweet chocolate chips

On your mark . . .

- Preheat the oven to 375°F with a rack in the middle slot of the oven.
- Lightly butter two 18 by 13-inch baking sheets or line them with parchment paper.

Get set . . .

- Combine the flour, baking soda, and salt in a large bowl, whisk to mix, and set aside.

Cook!

- Melt the butter and peanut butter in a medium-size saucepan over low heat. Add the raw sugar and stir until the ingredients are melted and combined. Remove the butter-and-sugar mixture from the heat and let cool for 3 minutes.

- Combine eggs and the vanilla in a medium bowl. Add them, along with the butter mixture, to the flour mixture. Using an electric hand-mixer, beat on low speed until smooth.

- Add the chocolate chips and continue to beat on low speed until chunky dough is formed.

- Refrigerate the dough for 10 minutes or up to 1 hour.

- Scoop up a heaping tablespoon of the dough and roll it into a ball the size of a golf ball. Place the ball on the cookie sheet and slightly flatten the dough into a 2-inch round. Repeat with the dough until you have 12 cookies on the tray, spacing the cookies about 2 inches apart.

- Bake the cookies, one sheet at a time, for 12 to 15 minutes, or until lightly brown.

- Prepare the second sheet of cookies while the first one bakes.

- Allow the cookies to cool on the sheets for 5 minutes before using a spatula to remove them to a rack to finish cooling.

4ᵀᴴ OF JULY SHORTCAKE

Here is a red, white, and blue celebration on a plate. This classic dessert of strawberries, blueberries, and whipped cream layered between homemade shortcake is bound to get raves and bring fireworks to your table.

SERVES 4

SHORTCAKE

2 cups unbleached all-purpose flour

¼ cup raw (turbinado) sugar

4 teaspoons baking powder

½ teaspoon salt

5½ tablespoons chilled unsalted butter, plus 1 tablespoon butter, melted and cooled for brushing

1 large egg

¾ cup buttermilk

STRAWBERRIES

1 quart strawberries

1 tablespoon raw (turbinado) sugar

½ pint blueberries

WHIPPED CREAM

½ pint (1 cup) heavy cream

⅓ cup confectioners' sugar

On your mark . . .

- Preheat the oven to 450°F with a rack in the middle slot of the oven. Place a stainless steel or glass bowl in the freezer to chill for the whipped cream.

- Using a piece of wax paper and 1 teaspoon butter, lightly grease an 18 by 13-inch baking sheet.

In a food processor

- In the bowl of a food processor with the all-purpose metal blade in place, combine the flour, raw sugar, baking powder, and salt. Pulse 10 to 15 times to combine the ingredients together. Cut the chilled butter into ½-inch slices and add to the food processor. Pulse for about 15 seconds, or until the mixture resembles coarse crumbs. Add the egg and buttermilk. Process until the ingredients form a ball.

By hand

- Whisk together the flour, sugar, and baking powder in a large bowl. Cut the butter into ½-inch slices and add to the flour. Use your fingertips to break up the butter. Rub it into the dry ingredients until the lumps disappear and the ingredients combine to form coarse crumbs. Add the buttermilk and mix with a large spoon until the mixture becomes a soft dough.

Get set . . .

- Pull the dough from the bowl onto a floured countertop or cutting board. Sprinkle a little extra flour on the dough and knead for a few seconds to form a ball. Cover the dough with a clean towel. (For more about kneading, see page 104.)

- Wash the strawberries and remove the green stem tops. A teaspoon works best for this.

- Wash the blueberries, remove any stems, drain and set aside.

- Chop the strawberries into medium-size chunks and place in a bowl with the blueberries and raw sugar. Toss lightly and set aside.

- Lightly flour a rolling pin and roll the dough into a 10- to 12-inch circle about 1½ inches thick.

- Cut half the dough into 3-inch squares. Cut the other half into about 3-inch circles. Use a cookie cutter or a juice glass to make the circles. You should have 8 cut pieces in total. If you need more dough, you can gather up the leftover dough from the cuttings, form it into a ball, flour it, and roll it out again. Then cut more circles and squares.

- Lay the squares on the baking sheet, brush with the melted butter, and lay the circles on top of the squares. Brush the tops of the circles with the remaining butter.

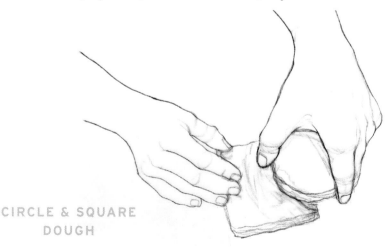

CIRCLE & SQUARE
DOUGH

Cook!

- Bake on the middle rack of the oven for 12 to 14 minutes, until the shortcakes are lightly browned.

- Lift them with a spatula, place onto a cooling rack, and let cool about for about 10 minutes.

- In the meantime, make the whipped cream. Pour the cream into the chilled stainless steel or glass bowl you put into the freezer earlier. Beat on high speed with an electric mixer. Rotate the bowl and move the beaters in a circle as you whip the cream to incorporate air into the cream as it thickens. Continue to beat the cream for 2 to 3 minutes until you see soft ridges on the surface of the cream.

- Turn off the mixer and lift the beaters out of the cream. If the cream clings to the beaters in soft clouds, it is done; if not, continue beating for another minute.

- Sift the confectioners' sugar over the cream with a hand-held strainer or flour sifter, gently shaking over the bowl. Use a rubber spatula to gently fold the sugar and cream together.

- Refrigerate the whipped cream until you are ready to serve.

- If you are serving the shortcakes immediately, separate the top circles from the bottom squares.

- Spoon on the berries and add a little cream, moistening the shortcake with some of the berry liquid. Serve immediately.

KITCHEN
ESSENTIALS

Anchovy fillets

This tiny fish packs a large punch of flavor. The anchovy is a very misunderstood ingredient in the kitchen and, unfortunately, often gets a negative response from people who are afraid to try it. When shopping, look for the anchovies in glass jars rather than in cans. They are already taken off the bone, are larger than the canned ones, and have better flavor. Rinse and pat the anchovies dry before you use them. If you have any left over, pack them back in the glass jar, cover with extra-virgin olive oil, and refrigerate.

Arugula

Arugula has been used in salads and sautés dating back to the Romans. The tender young leaves and stems have a light, peppery flavor. As the leaves mature, the flavor becomes stronger. For that reason, the younger leaves are generally preferred, though the more mature leaves are good in stir-fries. Arugula leaves can hold plenty of sand and dirt so it is essential that they are washed thoroughly before using.

Balsamic vinegar

This sweet and tangy vinegar is traditionally from the Emilia-Romagna region of northern Italy. Balsamic vinegar has been made in this region for over a thousand years. There are many grades of balsamic vinegar, and prices can vary from inexpensive to very costly. The natural sweetness of the grapes used to make balsamic vinegar, along with the natural bite that comes from fermentation, makes this vinegar very versatile and appealing.

Buckwheat flour

Read more about buckwheat flour on page 26.

Butter

Butter is made by churning heavy cream until it becomes smooth and almost solid. After the butter has been churned, it is washed to remove the buttermilk. This step improves the flavor and texture of butter, as well as increases its shelf life. It is more common to use unsalted butter in sweet pastries because salt can overpower the delicate flavor of fruits or fillings. Salted butter is more common in savory dishes.

Buttermilk

Originally buttermilk was the leftover liquid that occurred after the fat had been separated out in the butter-making process. Today the more readily available "cultured buttermilk" is actually skimmed milk that has been slightly fermented. Buttermilk is naturally low in fat and has a slightly sour flavor that many people find appealing.

Cayenne pepper

This pepper has very high heat content and is packed with seeds and fibers that contain a great deal of its power punch of hotness. It is believed that cayenne originated in South America and is named after the Cayenne River in French Guiana. The dried powder made from this pepper comes from varieties that grow in Louisiana, Africa, Mexico, and Japan.

Chervil

A green leafy herb that looks a little like parsley, chervil has a light, tangy flavor and works best in a dish when used fresh. If you can't find chervil, you can substitute an equal amount of fresh tarragon or flat-leaf parsley.

Chick peas

This legume is one of the oldest foods on the planet, dating back to 4000 BC, and is believed to be one of the first cultivated crops. The chick pea is a relative of the sweet pea. Dried chick peas can be ground into flour, or they can be cooked whole in water until softened and then used as an ingredient in appetizers, salads, and even desserts. The nutty, mild taste is very popular in Middle Eastern and Italian cooking. Chick peas also are known as garbanzo beans.

Chile powder

Red chile peppers are dried and blended with spices such as cumin, garlic powder, and salt to make chile powder. You can also find chile powder that has been smoked for maximum flavor.

Chipotle chiles in adobo sauce

Once jalapeño peppers are dried and smoked, they are called chipotles. Adobo sauce is made from tomatoes, vinegar, other chiles, and seasonings. The dried peppers are packed in the sauce and provide quite a hot wallop of flavor, so use them sparingly.

Chives

A member of the onion family, chives taste best when they are fresh and not dried. Their flavor is more delicate than onions. Chives are easy to grow and their appearance in a garden is usually the first sign of spring.

Cilantro

Cilantro is an herb also known as coriander or Chinese parsley. It adds great flavor to dishes. Cilantro looks almost identical to parsley and is easily confused with it, but it has a bolder flavor and a spicy aroma. It should be washed to remove any sand or dirt still clinging to the stems or leaves. Wrapped in wax paper or plastic wrap, it will keep for up to one week in the refrigerator.

Cornmeal

Cornmeal is coarse-ground flour made from dried corn kernels. It is a popular ingredient in Mexican cooking. It is available in white or yellow and has a coarse texture. It adds a distinctive crunch to the recipes in which it is used.

Corn tortillas

Mexican tortillas usually contain just corn flour (called masa) and water. Look for tortillas that are made without chemical preservatives or added fats. If you have a Mexican specialty store or well-stocked supermarket near you, chances are you will find excellent tortillas. Tortillas also freeze well. Thaw frozen tortillas before you attempt to separate them, or they are likely to split.

Ginger

Ginger, sometimes called gingerroot, is really a rhizome. When you shop for fresh ginger, look for firm texture and smooth skin with no dark spots or shriveled ends. Peel off the outer skin with a vegetable peeler. Crush ginger slices on a cutting board to release the pungent flavor. You can also use a grater, zester, or garlic press to extract the liquid. Ginger can add a lot of heat to your recipe, so use it sparingly.

Greek-style yogurt

A thick, rich yogurt made from strained whole milk, either cow's or sheep's milk, that separates the liquid from the whey. It is a great substitute for heavy cream.

Grits

In the southern United States, hominy grits—finely ground dried, white corn kernels—are sometimes referred to as "the potatoes of the South," a clear indication of their popularity.

Honey

This fragrant, naturally sweet, golden nectar of the honey bee has been around for thousands of years. When shopping for honey, look for local honey from your area. Honeys can be naturally flavored with lavender, thyme, wildflower, clove, and orange blossom, depending on where it was collected. You can sometimes also find honey still in the honeycomb. Remember to tightly seal the jar and to wipe the outside of it with a damp cloth to remove any drips before you put it in the cupboard. It is not necessary to refrigerate honey.

Jalapeños

The jalapeño is probably the most familiar of all chiles. This famous rich, green, hot pepper can be found in salsa and sauces. The jalapeño, which generally measures about 2½ inches long and ¾ inches wide, originated in Mexico. Available fresh or canned, it ranges from hot to very hot. You should handle it only with protective latex kitchen gloves. Remove the seeds and veins from the inside if you want to reduce its heat, or leave the seeds and veins if you want the pepper at its full heat.

Kiwi fruit

This green, fuzzy fruit has a sweet and tart-tangy flavor and is loaded with vitamin C. Growers in New Zealand made kiwis popular, but now they are grown in California as well. Wash and peel the outside skin before using kiwis in your recipe. Kiwis keep well for up to two weeks if kept in the coldest part of the refrigerator.

Maple syrup, pure

There is about a six-week window of time in late winter, when warm, sunny days and cold nights cause sap to flow in maple trees. The tree trunk is tapped with a spout and the maple sap drips into buckets. The collected sap is cooked down into syrup. The process is slow but worth the effort. Pure maple syrup is expensive because it is so time consuming to make; and it takes about 30 to 40 gallons of sap boiled down to make 1 gallon of maple syrup. Nearly 90 percent of Americans have never tasted the real thing. The imitation variety sold in supermarkets may contain as little as 2 percent actual maple syrup, or it may be made with all imitation ingredients. Pure maple syrup is graded by color and varies in flavor from delicate to robust.

Molasses

The dark, fragrant, sweet liquid comes from raw sugar after the sugar cane is crushed and the juice is extracted and boiled. The reduction process produces two products – raw sugar and molasses. Look for unsulfured or blackstrap molasses.

Mozzarella cheese

A delicate white cheese made from cow's or buffalo's milk, mozzarella melts wonderfully and is an important ingredient in many dishes, including pizza, salads, and sandwiches. If you buy it freshly made, use it within two days of purchase. If you buy it packaged, check the expiration date and choose the one with the date furthest from the purchase date.

Olive oil, extra-virgin

Olive oil is classified by the name "extra-virgin" if it has been obtained from the first pressing of the olives without the use of chemicals and has low acidity (less than one percent). It also has great flavor. If the oil is cold pressed, it means the olives were pressed without heat, so the oil keeps its flavor. In salad dressings, the flavor of good oil will greatly enhance any salad you make. The oil must be protected from sunlight and kept in a cool place. Check the expiration date on the oil before you purchase it. Buy oil with the furthest date from the day you are purchasing it.

Onion, Vidalia

This popular onion was first grown in Toombs County, Georgia, around 1940. It turned out to be sweet and not hot like most traditional onions. It took a while before it caught on, but now it has a huge following from devoted onion eaters. The Vidalia is the Georgia state vegetable. The onions are available from early April to late November. The Vidalia is so mild that onion connoisseurs say you can eat this onion like an apple. Store Vidalias in a cool, dry, place out of direct sunlight. Other sweet onions include the Maui from Hawaii and the Walla Walla onion from Washington State.

Panko

These Japanese bread crumbs are made from crust-less bread that is dried and ground to create coarse and crispy crumbs. Panko absorbs liquid and spices very well and still keeps its crunch. Look for panko crumbs that contain no partially hydrogenated oils or preservatives.

Paprika, smoked

A blend of fresh red peppers that are smoked over wood fires, then dried and ground. The paprika develops a rich taste with a hint of smoke and an appealing deep color.

Poppy seeds

The blue-gray seeds of the poppy plant are used whole, or pressed into oil. Poppy seeds have a mild flavor and can be used in salad dressings, sprinkled on breads and cakes before baking, and roasted and used in spice mixes.

Quinoa

Read more about quinoa on page 82.

Radicchio

A member of the chicory family, a head of radicchio is just a little larger than an orange. Its colorful, delicate, red and white lettuce-like leaves make it a great addition to any salad. Look for firm, solid heads with no wilted or brown leaves. Wash the leaves and pat them dry with paper towels or dry in a salad spinner. Tear the leaves rather than cut them with a knife. Belgian endive is a good substitute.

Red pepper flakes, crushed

Dried, hot red peppers are crushed into flakes. Red pepper flakes have plenty of heat so use them with caution.

Ricotta cheese

A delicate, light Italian cheese made from the whey that is the by-product of cheesemaking, ricotta is the equivalent of American cottage cheese. It can be purchased fresh, or mass produced. Fresh ricotta should be consumed within a few days of purchase. If buying packaged, be sure to check the expiration date and choose the date furthest from the day you are purchasing it.

Rye flour

Rye flour comes from a hearty grain and generally has a somewhat stronger flavor than wheat or oats. When used with wheat flour, it adds a distinct, slightly sour flavor and chewy texture to breads and pizza dough.

Safflower oil

The safflower is native to western Asia and is a cousin to the sunflower. It is naturally high in polyunsaturated fats and has a light, appealing flavor. Safflower oil is perishable and should be kept out of direct sun and refrigerated.

Sage

Sage is a cousin to mint and has a robust flavor. Sage is simple to grow and dries easily, making it a great choice for new gardeners. Sage enhances the flavor of pork, chicken, and turkey and is a common ingredient in savory bread stuffing.

Salt

Salt is produced by evaporating sea water and it is also mined from salt mines. It is probably the oldest and most common seasoning in cooking. Just enough of it can bring a dish together, and too much of it can ruin a recipe just as quickly. There are many varieties of unrefined, minimally processed salts, such as *fleur de sel* and other sea salts. A more processed and refined salt is commonly known as table salt, which may have iodine added (iodized). Another popular salt with chefs and home cooks alike is kosher salt, which has a coarse grind. It is available in most supermarkets.

Serrano chiles

The Serrano chile is packed with heat. It is smaller than the jalapeño and has a bullet shape. Its use is very common in Mexican cooking. Always wear gloves to protect your skin when handling fresh chiles.

Sesame seeds

These tiny, nutty, very flavorful seeds have been used for centuries. Sesame seeds may be white, black, yellow, or brown, and are often toasted for added flavor.

Spelt flour

Spelt flour is higher in protein, sweeter, and has a more pronounced nutty flavor than whole-wheat flour. Spelt contains a broad collection of nutrients and has gained new-found popularity in recent years not only for its taste, but for its supposed health benefits as well. Spelt dates back thousands of years and has been grown in the United States for the last hundred years. Spelt looks like wheat, but actually it is quite different. The outside husk is tougher, which protects its nutritional content. Some people with wheat allergies find it a good alternative. It does contain gluten, so it is not recommended for gluten-free recipes.

Sugar, raw

Turbinado sugar is an alternative to white, processed sugar. Raw sugar, like white sugar, is harvested from sugar cane, but it is less processed and contains a few less calories per teaspoon.

Sunflower seeds

The brilliant, golden sunflower certainly lives up to its name. At the center of the flour are the seeds that, when pressed, are prized for their oil. The seeds are also very popular because they are high in protein, rich in mono- and polyunsaturated fats, and filled with vitamins and minerals. The oil is perishable and should be kept in a dark, cool place once opened.

Tabasco sauce

Tabasco is the trade name for a bottled hot sauce that originated around 1870 and is made from Tabasco peppers. The sauce is actually fermented in large casks on Avery Island in Louisiana. The sauce is extremely hot; use it with caution and think of it as liquid heat.

Tahini paste

Tahini paste is extracted from sesame seeds, which are soaked in water for twenty-five hours and hammered to separate the bran from the seed kernels. The kernels are soaked again in salt water and grilled to bring out the flavor of the sesame seed. Then the seeds are sent to a mill to be crushed into creamy paste. Tahini paste is one of the main ingredients in hummus, a chick-pea spread. Its nutty flavor is similar to peanut butter, but it has a stronger taste.

Tofu

Read more about tofu on page 28.

Tomatillos

Tomatillos are a small, green, tart fruit. They are often confused with green tomatoes. The papery outer husk needs to be peeled away and removed before using, and then the fruit should be washed to remove any sticky residue. Look for firm, solid tomatillos that fill the skin completely. They will keep in the vegetable drawer in the refrigerator for several weeks.

Tomatoes, plum

Plum, sometimes called roma, tomatoes are available in supermarkets year-around. The tomato has a pear shape and does not contain a lot of seeds. When shopping for tomatoes, look for rich, red color and stay away from ones with dark spots or bruises. Ripen and store tomatoes at room temperature. A tomato will lose most of its flavor if stored in the refrigerator.

Turmeric, ground

India is the largest producer of turmeric in the world. A rhizome similar to ginger, turmeric is picked young, cleaned, and dried in the sun. It is then ground into a golden powder. Turmeric is used as a fabric dye as well as a spice. Be careful! It will stain, and the stains are not easy to remove.

Vanilla extract, pure

Vanilla extract contains the flavor and delicate aroma of vanilla beans. The extract is blended with alcohol to preserve its delicate flavor. If possible, look for pure vanilla extract rather than imitation vanilla for the recipes in this book. Pure vanilla is generally more expensive than imitation, so you should keep your budget in mind when selecting.

Whole-wheat flour

Whole-wheat flour contains the whole kernel of wheat ground into flour. As a result it retains more nutrients than bleached white flour. It can give breads and pastries more density and has a nuttier taste than lighter flours.

You can use the chart below to convert from U.S. measurements to the metric system.

Weight

1 ounce = 28 grams

½ pound (8 ounces) = 227 grams

1 pound = .45 kilogram

2.2 pounds = 1 kilogram

Liquid volume

1 teaspoon = 5 milliliters

1 tablespoon = 15 milliliters

1 fluid ounce = 30 milliliters

1 cup = 240 milliliters (.24 liter)

1 pint = 480 milliliters (.48 liter)

1 quart = 950 milliliters (.95 liter)

Length

¼ inch = .6 centimeter

½ inch = 1.25 centimeters

1 inch = 2.5 centimeters

Temperature

100°F = 40°C

110°F = 45°C

212°F = 100°C (boiling point of water)

350°F = 180°C

375°F = 190°C

400°F = 200°C

425°F = 220°C

450°F = 235°C

(To convert temperatures in Fahrenheit to Celsius, subtract 32 and multiply by .56)

METRIC CONVERSION CHART

BAKING SHEETS

CAST-IRON SKILLET

FONDUE POT

BAKING SHEET
(WITH 1-INCH SIDES)

COLANDER

FOOD PROCESSOR

BLENDER

CUTTING BOARD

FOUR-SIDED GRATER

CAKE PAN, 9X13-INCH

DEEP-DISH PIZZA PAN

JUICER

CASSEROLE DISH

ELECTRIC HAND-MIXER

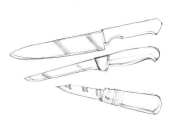

KNIVES, ASSORTED

LATEX GLOVES

MUFFIN TIN, 6-CUP

RUBBER SPATULA

MEASURING CUPS

PANCAKE GRIDDLE

SAUCEPANS WITH LIDS,
ASSORTED SIZES

MEASURING SPOONS

PASTRY BRUSH

LARGE METAL SLOTTED SPOON

MEAT THERMOMETER OR INSTANT-
READ THERMOMETER

ROASTING PAN

SOUFFLÉ DISH

MIXING BOWLS, ASSORTED

ROLLING PIN

SPATULA

STANDARD PIZZA PAN

TONGS

WIRE POTATO MASHER

STOCK POT

VEGETABLE/POTATO PEELER

WOODEN SPOONS

STRAINER

WHISK

10-INCH ROUND PIE
PAN/BAKING DISH

WIRE COOLING RACK

Index